Chapter 1: Introduction to the World of Panic Attacks

Panic attacks are sudden and intense bursts of fear accompanied by physical symptoms and a sense of losing control over oneself. These attacks can strike unexpectedly: while walking in the park, driving a car, or even at home, in what seems like a safe environment. The fear experienced in these moments feels so real and overwhelming that it's hard to believe in its psychological nature.

A panic attack is not just "severe stress" or "nervous tension." It is a powerful bodily reaction that affects physiological processes and alters one's perception of the world. People who suffer from panic attacks often describe them as a sense of impending doom, an imminent fear of death, or a complete loss of control over their body and mind. For many, these episodes become a significant obstacle in daily life, hindering normal activities and reducing quality of life.

Why Is This Topic Important?

In today's fast-paced and increasingly stressful world, the topic of panic attacks has immense relevance. It is estimated that up to 4% of people worldwide experience panic attacks at least once in their lifetime. These episodes can affect individuals of any age or gender, although women and young adults are more frequently affected. Despite their prevalence, panic attacks remain shrouded in myths and misunderstandings.

For some, a panic attack may be a one-time occurrence triggered by extreme stress. For others, it can become a chronic issue that requires serious attention and a strategic approach to treatment. Sometimes, panic attacks evolve into more severe conditions, such as panic disorder or agoraphobia, where a person becomes afraid to leave home due to the fear of having another attack.

The History of Panic Research

Historically, panic attacks were viewed as signs of "hysteria" or something that happened to emotionally unstable individuals. However, the scientific approach to studying panic only began to emerge relatively recently. In the late 20th century, researchers and doctors began to explore how physiology, psychology, and stress contribute to these episodes.

Understanding the nature of panic attacks has been key to developing treatments and support for those who suffer from them. We now recognize that panic is not a sign of weakness but a result of a complex interaction between the mind and body. It is a reaction rooted in human evolution, where a quick burst of adrenaline in the blood could save a life in dangerous situations.

Goals of This Book

The goal of this book is to help you understand what a panic attack is, how and why it occurs, and, most importantly, what you can do about it. We will explore the causes and mechanisms behind panic, examine the symptoms, and look into different treatment methods. But above all, we will learn how to regain control and live a full life without the fear of another attack.

The knowledge you gain from this book will not only benefit those who suffer from panic attacks but also their loved ones, who often feel powerless in the face of their loved one's suffering. Understanding what is happening and how to fix it provides enormous potential for personal growth, healing, and a return to normal life.

Personal Awareness

Remember, you are not alone. Millions of people worldwide face the same symptoms and experiences as you. Many have managed to overcome panic attacks, find ways to manage their condition, and regain the joy of life. This book is your guide to understanding yourself and your reactions, a guide to healing and peace.

_About the Book__:_
This book is a comprehensive guide to understanding, managing, and recovering from panic attacks. It provides insight into the biological, psychological, and emotional aspects of panic, offering practical tools for coping and long-term strategies for maintaining mental health. Whether you're currently struggling with panic attacks or looking to support someone else, this book serves as both a resource and an inspiration. Through detailed chapters, you'll learn the science behind panic, the triggers that set it off, and the psychological cycles that make it difficult to break free. You'll discover effective techniques such as mindfulness, cognitive behavioral therapy (CBT), and stress management practices that empower you to take control of your mental health.
The book also tackles the social and emotional impacts of panic attacks, offering support for relationships, feelings of shame, and isolation. In the final chapters, you'll read real-life success stories of individuals who have overcome their struggles, along with strategies for continued healing and emotional well-being.
This is more than just a guide; it's a companion for your journey towards a life free from the grip of panic.

Table of Contents

The Science of Panic: Understanding the Mechanisms

A panic attack is much more than just a feeling of fear or extreme anxiety. It is a complex physiological and psychological process that involves the entire body in response to a perceived threat. To better understand the nature of panic, it is important to explore how biological and psychological mechanisms interact to create the conditions for this state.

The Biological Roots of Panic

On a biological level, a panic attack is part of the "fight or flight" response, an evolutionary survival mechanism. This reaction was crucial for our ancestors when facing dangerous situations. For example, when confronted with a wild animal, the body would instantly mobilize: the heart would beat faster to supply blood to the muscles, breathing would quicken to saturate the blood with oxygen, and the release of adrenaline and cortisol would help focus and prepare to either run or fight.

However, in the modern world, real survival threats are much rarer. Nevertheless, this ancient protective system remains active and can respond to any stressor that the brain perceives as a threat, even if there is no actual danger. The problem is that the brain and body often struggle to distinguish between real and imagined threats. As a result, ordinary situations – such as taking an exam, attending a tense meeting, or even riding in crowded transportation – can trigger the same intense physiological response as facing a wild animal.

The Role of the Nervous System

The autonomic nervous system, which consists of the sympathetic and parasympathetic systems, plays a central role in this process. The sympathetic nervous system activates in moments of danger, increasing heart rate, raising blood pressure, and triggering sweating. These are the same symptoms people feel during a panic attack: rapid heartbeat, shortness of breath, trembling, and sweating.

The parasympathetic nervous system, on the other hand, is responsible for calming the body and restoring it after stress. In people prone to panic attacks, there is sometimes an imbalance between these systems, causing the sympathetic system to activate too often or too intensely.

The Neurochemistry of Panic

Brain chemicals like serotonin, norepinephrine, and gamma-aminobutyric acid (GABA) also play a key role in panic. Norepinephrine, a neurotransmitter associated with the stress response, can trigger panic symptoms when overly activated. Serotonin, in contrast, helps regulate mood and emotions, and a deficiency can contribute to heightened anxiety.

Research has shown that an imbalance in the brain's neurochemical systems can increase the likelihood of panic attacks. Some people are genetically predisposed to having a brain that reacts more intensely to stress. This explains why panic attacks can run in families and why they often first appear in adolescence or early adulthood, when the brain is particularly sensitive to stress.

Psychological Aspects of Panic

Psychological factors also play a significant role in the emergence of panic. Thoughts and perceptions influence how a person interprets their physical symptoms. For example, if someone feels their heart racing and immediately thinks, "I'm dying" or "I'm having a heart attack," the fear intensifies, triggering a full-blown panic attack. This catastrophic thinking sets off a cycle of fear that only worsens the symptoms.

Past experiences can also influence how one responds to stress. If someone has experienced a traumatic event or a panic attack before, the brain may remember this as a dangerous situation and react similarly in the future, even to minor signs of threat. Additionally, stressful life events, such as losing a loved one, financial difficulties, or other major changes, can contribute to the development of panic attacks.

The Interaction of Biological and Psychological Mechanisms

Panic is the result of the interaction between biology and psychology. For instance, stress or a negative thought can trigger a bodily reaction that leads to a panic attack. Conversely, experiencing a strong physiological response can lead to anxious thoughts and beliefs, creating a vicious cycle of fear.

This explains why treating panic attacks often requires a comprehensive approach. Pharmacotherapy helps address chemical imbalances, while psychological methods like cognitive-behavioral therapy teach people to change their thinking and perception of symptoms.

Why This Knowledge Matters

Understanding how the mechanisms of panic work can significantly ease the struggle with this condition. When a person realizes that their symptoms are a natural bodily reaction, not a life-threatening situation, they begin to feel more in control. This awareness becomes the first step toward recovery and a return to a full and healthy life.

: **Symptoms: When the Body Cries for Help**

Panic attacks can manifest with a wide range of physical and psychological symptoms, which often come on suddenly and without warning. For those experiencing a panic attack, these symptoms can be overwhelming and terrifying, making it difficult to recognize that they are part of an intense but temporary reaction. Understanding these symptoms and why they occur is crucial in helping individuals manage their panic attacks more effectively.

Physical Symptoms

One of the most distressing aspects of a panic attack is the physical response, which is a result of the body's "fight or flight" mechanism. These symptoms are so intense that many people believe they are experiencing a medical emergency. Here are some of the most common physical manifestations:

Rapid Heartbeat (Palpitations): The heart races or pounds in the chest, which can feel like an impending heart attack. This is the body's way of pumping more blood to prepare the muscles for a quick response.

Shortness of Breath: A feeling of being unable to breathe deeply or a sensation of suffocation. The lungs try to take in more oxygen as part of the body's preparation for dealing with danger.

Chest Pain or Discomfort: This can feel like tightness, pressure, or a sharp pain. Many people mistake this symptom for a heart attack, which increases the level of fear.

Dizziness or Lightheadedness: A sense of vertigo or feeling faint can be caused by hyperventilation or a sudden drop in blood pressure.

Sweating: Excessive sweating, often cold and clammy, occurs as the body tries to regulate its temperature in response to perceived danger.

Shaking or Trembling: The muscles tense up, causing the body to shake uncontrollably. This is another way the body prepares to act quickly.

Hot Flashes or Chills: Changes in body temperature are common, as the nervous system reacts to stress.

Nausea or Stomach Upset: The digestive system slows down during a panic attack, causing nausea, abdominal discomfort, or a sensation of a "knot" in the stomach.

Numbness or Tingling (Paresthesia): A sensation of pins and needles, often in the hands or feet, is caused by changes in blood flow or hyperventilation.

Feeling of Choking: A sensation that the throat is closing or that something is stuck, making swallowing difficult.

These physical symptoms are the body's way of preparing to deal with a threat, even if the threat is not real. They are intense but typically not harmful, although the experience can be extremely frightening.

Psychological Symptoms

Alongside physical symptoms, panic attacks are often accompanied by a range of psychological experiences that heighten the sense of fear and make the episode even more distressing. Here are some common psychological symptoms:

Overwhelming Fear: This can be a fear of losing control, going crazy, or even dying. The sense of impending doom feels very real in the moment.

Detachment or Unreality (Derealization and Depersonalization): Some people feel disconnected from their surroundings or as though they are observing themselves from the outside, as if in a dream. This adds to the feeling of losing control.

Intense Anxiety: A sudden wave of anxiety that peaks rapidly, often within minutes. This anxiety can feel unmanageable and all-consuming.

Confusion and Disorientation: It can be hard to think clearly or make sense of what is happening, leading to feelings of helplessness and distress.

Hyperawareness of Bodily Sensations: During a panic attack, people become acutely aware of their physical symptoms, which can exacerbate the fear and lead to a cycle of escalating anxiety.

The Experience of a Panic Attack

A panic attack usually lasts for about 10 to 20 minutes, though the peak of intensity often occurs within the first 10 minutes. For some, the symptoms may last longer or occur in waves. The combination of physical and psychological symptoms can make it difficult to believe that the experience will pass, which often contributes to an ongoing sense of dread and worry about future attacks.

Why the Body Reacts This Way

Understanding that these symptoms are the result of the body's natural stress response can help reduce the fear surrounding them. The body is simply trying to protect itself, even if the threat is imagined or misinterpreted. Recognizing that these intense sensations are temporary and not life-threatening is a critical step in learning to cope with panic attacks.

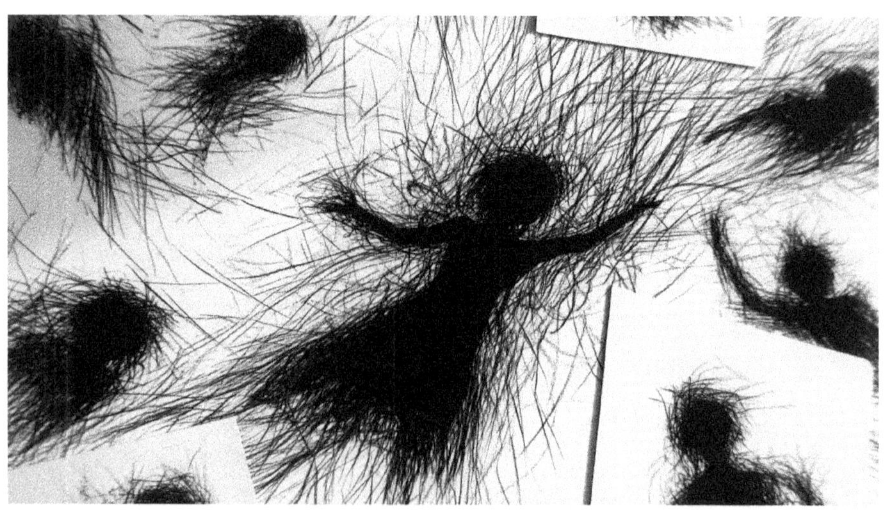

Triggers and Triggers Mechanisms: What Triggers Panic Attacks and How to Recognize Them

A panic attack is a sudden, intense experience of fear or anxiety that can manifest physically and emotionally. These attacks are often accompanied by symptoms such as rapid heartbeat, sweating, shortness of breath, dizziness, nausea, and a feeling of fear that may not be linked to any specific situation. It's important to understand that panic attacks can be triggered by various factors, which are the triggers or mechanisms that set them off.

What is a Trigger?

A trigger is any external or internal event that initiates a panic attack. It can be a specific situation, object, place, or even a physical or emotional state. For example, a person who has experienced trauma may start feeling a panic attack when faced with a reminder of that event.

Triggers can be both obvious and hidden. For instance, if someone has been in a car accident, traveling by car might become a trigger for a panic attack. Or, they might be more abstract factors like stress or life changes, which can provoke intense anxiety without a clear connection to a specific event.

Common Types of Panic Attack Triggers

Physical Sensations:

Some physical symptoms, such as rapid heartbeat, sweating, or dizziness, may be interpreted by the person as signs of an impending panic attack. When the person begins to experience these symptoms, it can intensify their anxiety and lead to panic. This can be related to a "misinterpretation" of bodily sensations, where normal physical reactions are perceived as life-threatening.

Emotional Stress:

Intense emotional experiences, such as the loss of a loved one, divorce, losing a job, or other significant life changes, can serve as powerful triggers for panic attacks. Ongoing stress at work or in personal life can also heighten anxiety, which increases the likelihood of panic attacks.

Social Situations:

Some people experience panic attacks in social situations, such as public speaking, interacting with strangers, or in crowded places. This is often related to phobias, such as social phobia or agoraphobia.

Traumatic Memories:

People who have experienced traumatic events, such as violence, war, accidents, or natural disasters, may experience panic attacks when faced with reminders of the incident. These reminders can be visual, auditory, or even smells, which activate fear and panic.

Phobias:

Panic attacks are often linked to phobias, which are irrational and intense fears of specific objects or situations. For example, the fear of heights (acrophobia), the fear of confined spaces (claustrophobia), or the fear of spiders (arachnophobia) can trigger panic attacks.

Physical Health:
Some illnesses and physical conditions can be associated with panic attacks. For instance, hypoglycemia (low blood sugar), thyroid problems, cardiovascular issues, or respiratory diseases can cause symptoms similar to a panic attack or exacerbate it.

Panic Attack Triggers Mechanisms
A trigger mechanism is the condition or factor that directly initiates a panic attack. It can be both an external stimulus (such as a specific situation) and internal (such as an emotional state). Trigger mechanisms often include:

Fear of a Recurrent Attack:
People who have experienced one panic attack may begin to fear that it will happen again, especially in situations where they felt anxious before. This fear can trigger further attacks, even if the situation itself poses no actual danger.

Feeling of Helplessness:
When a person feels unable to control a situation or their emotions, it can provoke a sense of panic. For example, if a person feels they cannot cope with the pressure at work or in personal life, it may lead to panic.

Exaggerated Response to Anxiety:
When a person starts to experience anxiety or discomfort, their perception of these feelings can become overly negative. Thoughts like "something is wrong with me," "I'm losing control," or "I'm going to die" can trigger a panic cycle.

Changes in Breathing:
Shallow or rapid breathing can be a trigger for a panic attack. When a person starts breathing faster or more shallowly due to stress, it can lead to hyperventilation, causing dizziness and a feeling of suffocation, which increases anxiety.

Alcohol, Drugs, and Caffeine:
The consumption of certain substances can trigger panic attacks. For example, caffeine and alcohol can increase anxiety levels, and drugs (especially stimulants) can cause strong physiological reactions that feel like panic.

Negative Thoughts and Catastrophizing:
When a person starts to exaggerate threats or interpret events negatively, it can trigger a panic attack. For example, thoughts like "something bad is going to happen," "I'm losing control," or "I'm going to die" can activate anxiety reactions.

How to Recognize a Panic Attack
Recognizing a panic attack is important in order to seek the necessary help and begin working on anxiety issues. Here are some signs to look for:

Physical Symptoms:
Rapid heartbeat, sweating, trembling, dizziness, shortness of breath, chest pain. There is often a feeling of losing control or "going crazy."

Psychological Symptoms:
A sense of fear, anxiety, worry, or even a "foreboding sense of death." Disorientation or a feeling that reality is unreal (depersonalization, derealization).

Duration:
A panic attack can last from a few minutes to half an hour. It usually starts suddenly and without a clear cause, although it may be influenced by stressful situations.

Panic Cycle: The Closed Loop of Fear

A panic attack is an intense episode of fear or anxiety that can occur unexpectedly, triggering a wide range of physical and emotional symptoms. However, for many individuals, panic attacks become part of a closed loop of fear, amplifying their intensity and duration. This cycle consists of several stages, each contributing to the next, increasing the level of fear and anxiety, and making it more difficult for the person to break free from this state.

In this article, we will take a detailed look at how the panic cycle works, its key stages, and ways to break free from it.

What is the Panic Cycle?

The panic cycle is a process in which one panic attack triggers the next, ultimately leading to a state of chronic fear and anxiety. It's a kind of "vicious circle" where each stage supports and strengthens the next, creating the threat of repeated attacks and complicating a person's ability to break out of this state.

The cycle begins with the normal experience of anxiety or stress, but quickly transitions into a panic attack, which can be even more frightening and unpredictable. This causes the person to avoid situations or places where they might experience subsequent attacks, which in turn only exacerbates the problem.

Stages of the Panic Cycle

Stress or Anxiety:

Everything begins when the individual experiences stress or anxiety, which may be triggered by external circumstances (such as work, relationships, or health issues). These feelings are completely normal in everyday life, but for people prone to panic attacks, they can quickly escalate.

Even normal physical stress symptoms, such as a racing heartbeat or increased sweating, can trigger anxiety. In this case, the person may begin to worry that these symptoms might lead to something more serious, such as a health emergency, or cause them to lose control.

Physiological Reactions:

In response to stress, the body activates the "fight or flight" response, a physiological reaction that increases the release of adrenaline and other stress hormones. This leads to an increased heart rate, shortness of breath, dizziness, and muscle tension. These symptoms can be frightening, especially if the person doesn't understand that they are a natural reaction of the body to stress. They begin to interpret these sensations as signs of a serious threat, which escalates their fear.

Interpreting Anxiety as a Threat:

When a person experiences stress symptoms (such as a racing heartbeat, sweating, dizziness), they start to interpret them as signs of something more dangerous. For example, they might think they are having a heart attack, losing consciousness, or that their life is in danger.

These thoughts and beliefs intensify the feeling of fear and anxiety. Instead of relaxing, the person becomes more convinced that their condition is worsening, which leads to the next stage — the panic attack.

Panic Attack:

A panic attack is an intense episode of fear, usually accompanied by rapid heartbeat, shortness of breath, dizziness, sweating, a feeling of choking, or fear of death. The symptoms can be so severe that the person may feel they are dying or going insane. Panic attacks typically start suddenly and can last from several minutes to half an hour. They are the climax of the cycle, confirming the person's fears and causing a sense of helplessness.

After the Attack — Worry About Recurrence:

After a panic attack, the person often experiences strong anxiety about it happening again. This may lead to a fear of specific situations or places where they have previously experienced a panic attack.

For example, if a panic attack occurred in a crowded place or on public transport, the person may begin to avoid these places, fearing that the attack will recur. This amplifies their anxiety and sense of isolation.

Avoiding Situations and Places:

People suffering from panic attacks may begin to avoid specific situations or places where they have experienced these attacks before. This might involve avoiding travel on public transport, crowded places, or other aspects of life related to social interaction.

Avoidance can offer temporary relief from anxiety, but it only strengthens the cyclical nature of panic. The more the person avoids situations, the stronger their fears become.

Increasing Fear and Depression:

Avoiding situations that could trigger a panic attack only increases the fear and anxiety. The person may feel increasingly isolated, detached, and helpless, which leads to elevated stress levels and depression.

This can also lead to restrictions in social life, professional activity, and even the development of phobias, such as agoraphobia (fear of open spaces) or social phobia (fear of social interaction).

How to Break the Panic Cycle?
Understanding how the panic cycle works is key to breaking it. Here are a few methods that can help individuals break free from this cycle:
Awareness and Acceptance of Symptoms:
The first step in breaking the cycle is to understand that the symptoms of anxiety and panic attacks are temporary and harmless. When the person learns to see them as a natural bodily reaction to stress, it reduces their fear.
Relaxation and Breathing Techniques:
Using breathing techniques (such as deep, slow breathing) helps to control the physical symptoms of panic and calm the nervous system. Relaxation practices like yoga or meditation can also help reduce overall anxiety levels.
Cognitive Behavioral Therapy (CBT):
CBT helps individuals change negative thoughts and beliefs that contribute to panic attacks. This involves reframing catastrophic thoughts that amplify fear and replacing them with more realistic and positive ones.
Exposure Therapy:
This method involves gradually and safely exposing the person to situations that previously triggered fear. It helps the person become desensitized to these situations and reduces fear levels over time.
Psychological Support:
Consulting with a psychologist or therapist can help individuals learn to manage anxiety and fear better, as well as address the root causes of panic attacks. In some cases, medication may be recommended to manage symptoms.
Conclusion
The panic cycle is a process in which one panic attack triggers the next, making them more frequent and intense. However, with the right treatment methods such as cognitive behavioral therapy, breathing techniques, and psychological support, it's possible to break free from this cycle and learn to control reactions to stress and anxiety. It's important to remember that panic attacks are temporary, and they can be overcome with the right approach and support.

Fear of Your Own Body: Panic Disorder Phobia

How Fear of Symptoms Intensifies Panic Attacks

Panic disorder is a condition where an individual experiences recurrent panic attacks, often without any clear external trigger. These attacks can be overwhelming and terrifying, as they involve a sudden surge of intense fear or discomfort. However, for some individuals, the fear of the physical symptoms associated with a panic attack—such as a racing heartbeat, dizziness, or shortness of breath—becomes a major trigger for future attacks. This phenomenon, often referred to as "fear of fear" or "fear of symptoms," can lead to a cycle where the person's anxiety about experiencing bodily sensations actually amplifies the occurrence of panic attacks. In this article, we will explore how the fear of bodily sensations plays a central role in panic disorder, how it contributes to the intensity of panic attacks, and ways to address and break the cycle of fear.

What is Fear of Symptoms?

Fear of symptoms refers to the anxiety and dread that individuals experience when they perceive or anticipate bodily sensations associated with panic attacks. These physical sensations—such as a racing heart, dizziness, difficulty breathing, or a feeling of choking—are often interpreted as signs of imminent danger, such as a heart attack or a life-threatening health issue. This misunderstanding can increase the individual's sense of fear and make the body's natural responses to stress even more distressing.

For someone with panic disorder, even mild physical discomfort can be perceived as a symptom of something far more serious, triggering a full-blown panic attack. This fear of experiencing the symptoms again can become so overwhelming that it perpetuates the cycle of panic attacks, where the fear of the next attack is as frightening as the attack itself.

How Fear of Symptoms Triggers Panic Attacks

Misinterpretation of Physical Sensations:
Panic attacks often begin with a normal, everyday physical sensation, such as a slightly elevated heart rate or muscle tension. However, for someone with panic disorder, these sensations may be misinterpreted as signs of a more serious health issue, such as a heart attack, stroke, or suffocation. The mind quickly jumps to catastrophic conclusions, fueling the fear and increasing anxiety, which in turn heightens the physical symptoms.

Hyperawareness of the Body:
People with panic disorder often become hyper-aware of any changes in their body. Every slight shift in heart rate, temperature, or breathing pattern is scrutinized, leading to increased anxiety about what it might mean. This heightened sensitivity to bodily sensations can cause an individual to be on edge constantly, worrying that any physical feeling might lead to a panic attack. As anxiety increases, so do the physical symptoms, triggering a cycle of fear.

Physical Sensations as a Threat:
The very sensations that occur during a panic attack—such as shortness of breath, chest tightness, or dizziness—are often interpreted as signs of imminent danger. This reaction makes the body's natural fight-or-flight response even more intense. The individual's attempt to escape or avoid these sensations only increases their fear, causing the body to respond more strongly, which can escalate the panic attack.

Avoidance Behavior:
As individuals with panic disorder begin to associate certain physical sensations with panic attacks, they may start avoiding situations or activities that they believe could trigger these symptoms. For example, someone who feels dizzy during a panic attack might avoid physical exercise or crowded places for fear that the dizziness will return. This avoidance behavior only strengthens the cycle, as the fear of experiencing the symptoms intensifies with each avoidance.

Anticipatory Anxiety:
In the period between panic attacks, individuals with panic disorder often experience anticipatory anxiety. They may constantly worry about when the next panic attack will happen, and the fear of experiencing the physical symptoms again becomes a dominant thought. This constant fear of the symptoms can create a constant state of anxiety, further increasing the likelihood of another panic attack.

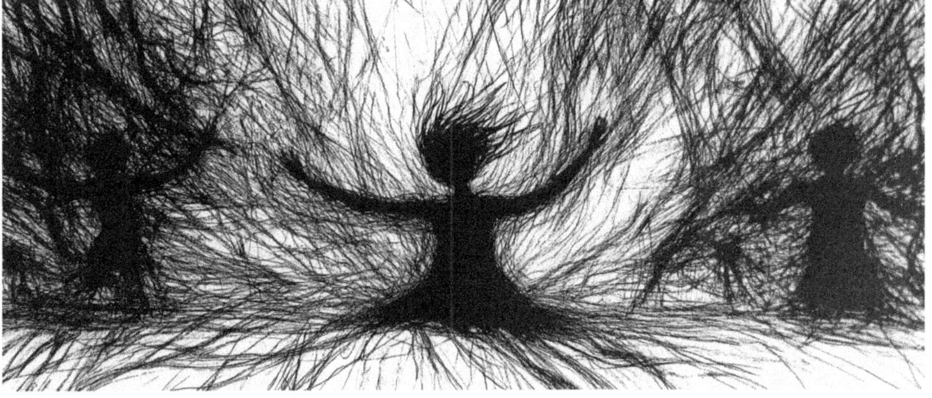

How the Fear of Symptoms Intensifies Panic Attacks

The fear of bodily sensations creates a self-reinforcing cycle. When a person experiences a normal physical sensation and interprets it as a potential panic attack, the fear generated by this interpretation causes even more physical symptoms. This intensifies the fear, making the individual feel even more out of control. The cycle works as follows:

Body Sensation: A normal physical sensation occurs, such as a slightly faster heart rate, a twinge of dizziness, or shortness of breath.

Interpretation: The individual misinterprets this sensation as a sign of something catastrophic, such as a heart attack or a life-threatening event.

Fear Response: The person becomes scared, which causes their body to react with even more intense symptoms. Their heart rate may speed up, they may begin to hyperventilate, and their muscles may tense up.

Panic Attack: The fear leads to a full-blown panic attack, with intense symptoms like rapid heartbeat, chest pain, dizziness, and difficulty breathing.

Reinforcement: After the panic attack subsides, the person is left with an even stronger fear of the next attack. They now associate the symptoms with something dangerous, which causes them to worry more about future attacks, starting the cycle over again.

Breaking the Cycle of Fear

Understanding how the fear of symptoms contributes to panic attacks is the first step in breaking the cycle. Here are some strategies to help individuals cope with their fear and reduce the frequency and intensity of panic attacks:

Education and Reassurance:

Learning that the physical sensations associated with panic attacks are not life-threatening can help reduce fear. Understanding that the body's response is natural and temporary can help individuals feel more in control and less afraid of their own physical sensations.

Mindfulness and Relaxation Techniques:

Mindfulness practices can help individuals observe their bodily sensations without judgment or fear. Learning to focus on the present moment, rather than catastrophizing future attacks, can reduce anticipatory anxiety. Relaxation techniques, such as deep breathing or progressive muscle relaxation, can help calm the body's response to stress.

Cognitive Behavioral Therapy (CBT):

CBT is an effective treatment for panic disorder. It helps individuals identify and challenge the negative thoughts and beliefs that contribute to the fear of symptoms. By reframing these thoughts, individuals can learn to perceive their bodily sensations in a less threatening way.

Gradual Exposure:

Gradual exposure to situations that may trigger panic symptoms can help individuals become desensitized to the sensations and reduce their fear over time. Starting with less anxiety-provoking situations and slowly working up to more challenging ones can help individuals gain confidence in managing their panic attacks.

Breathing Exercises:

Deep breathing exercises help regulate the body's response to stress. By focusing on slow, deep breaths, individuals can counteract the physical symptoms of panic, such as shortness of breath or dizziness, and bring their anxiety levels down.

Panic and Your Brain: The Neuropsychology of Fear

How the Brain Responds to Threats and How Reactive States Differ

Panic attacks are intense, sudden surges of fear and anxiety that often come without warning. These attacks can be overwhelming and physically distressing, leaving individuals feeling out of control. Understanding the neuropsychology of fear helps to explain why panic attacks happen and how the brain responds to perceived threats. In this article, we will explore how the brain processes fear, the different states that can trigger panic, and how these responses affect the body and mind.

How the Brain Responds to Threats: The Fear Response

The brain's response to perceived threats is part of an ancient survival mechanism known as the "fight-or-flight" response. This response is triggered by the brain when it detects danger, preparing the body to either confront the threat (fight) or escape from it (flight). The fear response is initiated by various structures in the brain, most notably the amygdala, which is responsible for detecting emotional significance in stimuli and activating the body's defense mechanisms.

The Amygdala:

The amygdala is the central hub of the brain's fear response. When you perceive a threat—whether physical, emotional, or psychological—the amygdala processes this information and signals the hypothalamus to trigger the body's physical responses. These can include an increase in heart rate, rapid breathing, muscle tension, and the release of stress hormones like adrenaline and cortisol. The amygdala also communicates with the prefrontal cortex, which helps assess the level of threat and determine an appropriate response.

The Prefrontal Cortex:

The prefrontal cortex plays a role in moderating the fear response by evaluating the threat. It is involved in decision-making and helps distinguish between real threats and false alarms. In people with anxiety or panic disorders, this area may be less effective at regulating the amygdala's response, leading to an exaggerated fear response.

The Hypothalamus:

Once the amygdala signals a threat, the hypothalamus activates the sympathetic nervous system (SNS), which is responsible for the "fight-or-flight" response. The SNS triggers physiological changes in the body, such as the release of adrenaline, increased heart rate, and shallow breathing, all of which prepare the body to react quickly to the perceived danger.

The Hippocampus:

The hippocampus plays a key role in memory formation and helps the brain recognize patterns or cues that may signal danger. It stores memories of previous threatening events, allowing the brain to respond more efficiently to similar situations in the future. However, in cases of chronic anxiety or panic disorder, the hippocampus can become hyperactive, leading to heightened sensitivity to perceived threats.

Reactive States: Understanding the Difference Between Normal and Abnormal Responses

The brain's fear response can be triggered in both normal and abnormal situations. However, the way the brain reacts in these states can differ significantly.

Normal Fear Response:

In healthy individuals, fear is a normal and adaptive response to actual threats. For example, if you are walking in a dark alley and hear footsteps behind you, your amygdala will activate the fear response to prepare you to either fight or flee. This response is appropriate and protective, as it helps you stay alert to potential danger. Once the threat passes (for instance, the footsteps turn out to be harmless), your brain returns to a calm state.

Heightened Fear Response (Hyperarousal):

In individuals with anxiety disorders, the brain's fear response can become heightened and overactive. This may result in a condition known as hyperarousal, where the body remains in a state of heightened alertness even in the absence of an immediate threat. Hyperarousal is often associated with conditions like generalized anxiety disorder (GAD) and post-traumatic stress disorder (PTSD). In these states, the amygdala may be overly sensitive, triggering fear responses in situations where there is no real danger.

Panic Attacks:

A panic attack is an extreme form of the fear response, often occurring without any clear external trigger. During a panic attack, the brain interprets the body's natural stress responses (such as increased heart rate or rapid breathing) as signs of an imminent life-threatening event, even when no threat exists. This leads to a cascade of physiological symptoms, including dizziness, chest pain, shortness of breath, and a sense of impending doom. The brain's misinterpretation of bodily sensations as dangerous fuels the cycle of panic, making it difficult for the individual to regain control.

Fight-or-Flight and the Freeze Response:

The typical fight-or-flight response is not the only way the brain can react to fear. Some individuals may experience the "freeze" response, where the brain becomes temporarily immobilized in the face of perceived danger. This can happen when the brain is overwhelmed by fear or unable to decide whether to confront or escape the threat. The freeze response is common in situations of trauma and can be associated with disorders like PTSD.

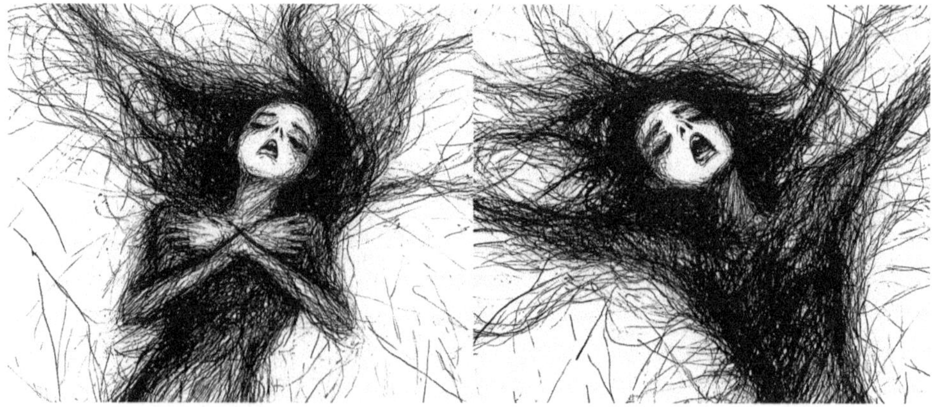

How Panic Affects the Body and Mind

The panic response involves a complex interaction between the brain and the body. Once the brain detects a threat and triggers the fear response, the body undergoes a series of physiological changes to prepare for action. These changes can be overwhelming and may include:

Physical Symptoms:

Panic attacks are often accompanied by physical symptoms such as a racing heart, chest tightness, shortness of breath, sweating, dizziness, trembling, and nausea. These symptoms are caused by the body's activation of the sympathetic nervous system, which prepares the body to deal with perceived danger.

Cognitive Symptoms:

The mind can also be affected during a panic attack. Cognitive symptoms may include feelings of detachment from reality, a sense of impending doom, or fear of losing control. The individual may have difficulty thinking clearly or rationally, as the brain's focus is entirely on the perceived threat.

Emotional Symptoms:

In addition to the physical and cognitive effects, panic attacks often cause intense emotional distress. The fear of dying, going crazy, or being unable to escape the situation can create lasting emotional turmoil. This emotional distress can persist even after the panic attack has subsided.

Hyperactivity of the Amygdala:

In people with panic disorder, the amygdala is often hyperactive, reacting more strongly to non-threatening stimuli. This hyperactivity makes it difficult for individuals to distinguish between real and perceived threats, leading to an exaggerated fear response. As a result, the brain's normal mechanisms for calming the body—such as the activation of the parasympathetic nervous system—may be delayed or ineffective.

The Role of Neurotransmitters

Neurotransmitters are chemicals in the brain that transmit signals between nerve cells. In individuals with panic disorder, the balance of neurotransmitters, particularly serotonin, dopamine, and gamma-aminobutyric acid (GABA), may be disrupted. These chemicals play a crucial role in regulating mood, anxiety, and the brain's response to stress.

Serotonin: Often called the "feel-good" neurotransmitter, serotonin helps regulate mood, anxiety, and fear responses. Low serotonin levels are commonly associated with anxiety and panic disorders.

Dopamine: Dopamine is involved in motivation and reward. Disruptions in dopamine signaling may contribute to the feeling of anxiety or dread that accompanies panic attacks.

GABA: GABA is the brain's primary inhibitory neurotransmitter, helping to calm the body and reduce the intensity of fear responses. A deficiency in GABA can lead to heightened anxiety and a more pronounced fear response.

First Aid for Panic Attacks: Practical Methods for Immediate Relief
Panic attacks can be overwhelming, often striking without warning and causing intense fear, confusion, and physical discomfort. When experiencing a panic attack, it can feel as though there's no escape from the fear and physical symptoms, such as a racing heart, dizziness, or shortness of breath. However, there are several effective techniques to alleviate symptoms and regain control during a panic attack. Below are practical methods for immediate relief, as well as strategies to prevent future episodes.

1. Breathing Techniques
One of the most common and effective ways to manage a panic attack is to control your breathing. During a panic attack, your breathing tends to become rapid and shallow, which can exacerbate feelings of anxiety and dizziness. By slowing down your breathing, you can help calm your nervous system and reduce physical symptoms.

How to Practice Deep Breathing:
Step 1: Find a quiet place where you can sit comfortably and focus.
Step 2: Breathe in slowly through your nose for a count of 4.
Step 3: Hold your breath for a count of 4.
Step 4: Exhale slowly through your mouth for a count of 6 or 8.
Step 5: Repeat this process several times until you start to feel calmer.
Deep breathing helps to increase the supply of oxygen to your brain, which helps to slow down the physical symptoms of a panic attack.

2. Grounding Techniques
During a panic attack, your mind may feel detached from reality, and you may feel as if you are losing control or about to faint. Grounding techniques help to bring you back to the present moment by focusing your attention on your physical surroundings and sensations.

How to Practice Grounding:

5-4-3-2-1 Technique:

This method uses your five senses to bring your awareness back to the present moment.

Look around and name 5 things you can see.

Identify 4 things you can touch.

Listen for 3 sounds you can hear.

Identify 2 smells you can detect (if possible).

Focus on 1 taste (perhaps a sip of water or chewing gum).

Focus on Your Feet:

Stand up (if possible) and press your feet firmly into the ground. Imagine the earth beneath you is supporting your weight. This can help to stabilize your body and mind.

3. Challenge Your Thoughts

Often, panic attacks are fueled by irrational thoughts or beliefs, such as "I'm dying" or "I can't breathe." These thoughts amplify the anxiety and make the attack worse. Learning to challenge these thoughts can help reduce the intensity of the attack.

How to Challenge Your Thoughts:

Identify the Thought: Acknowledge the negative or fearful thought that is causing anxiety.

Ask Yourself: Is this thought based on reality? What evidence do I have to support or challenge this thought?

Reframe the Thought: Replace the fearful thought with a more rational one. For example, "This is a panic attack, and it will pass" or "My body is just reacting to stress, but I'm not in danger."

By reframing your thoughts, you can reduce their power and prevent them from escalating the panic attack.

4. Relaxation Exercises

Progressive muscle relaxation (PMR) is a technique where you systematically tense and relax different muscle groups in your body to reduce physical tension and anxiety. This helps to shift the focus away from panic symptoms and brings your body back into a more relaxed state.

How to Practice Progressive Muscle Relaxation:

Step 1: Start by sitting or lying in a comfortable position. Close your eyes and take a few deep breaths.

Step 2: Begin with your feet. Tighten the muscles in your feet and hold for a few seconds, then relax them.

Step 3: Move upward through your body, tensing and relaxing each muscle group. Work your way from your legs to your abdomen, chest, hands, arms, neck, and face.

Step 4: As you relax each muscle group, focus on the sensation of release and relaxation.

This practice can help break the cycle of tension and panic by redirecting your mind and body toward relaxation.

Use a Calming Image or Visualization

Visualization techniques can be a powerful tool in calming the mind during a panic attack. By focusing on a calming image or scene, you can shift your attention away from the panic symptoms and towards something soothing.

How to Practice Visualization:

Step 1: Close your eyes and take a deep breath.

Step 2: Picture a peaceful, calming image, such as a beach, a forest, or a place that makes you feel safe and relaxed.

Step 3: Focus on all the details of the image—what you see, hear, feel, and smell.

Step 4: Stay with the visualization for several minutes until you begin to feel calmer.

Visualization helps to reframe the fear and anxiety, allowing your body and mind to shift from a heightened state of alertness to a more peaceful and relaxed one.

6. Reassure Yourself

It's common to feel like the panic attack will never end, but reminding yourself that panic attacks are temporary can help to ease some of the fear. Panic attacks usually peak within 10 minutes and start to subside afterward. Reassuring yourself that the feelings will pass can help to reduce the sense of impending doom.

How to Reassure Yourself:

Step 1: Remind yourself, "This is just a panic attack. I am not in any real danger."

Step 2: Think back to previous panic attacks you've experienced and how they eventually ended. Remind yourself that this one will pass too.

Step 3: Trust your ability to manage the situation and remind yourself that you have coping mechanisms in place.

7. Aromatherapy

Aromatherapy can be a helpful tool in calming the nervous system during a panic attack. Certain essential oils, such as lavender, chamomile, or peppermint, are known for their calming and stress-relieving properties. You can use an essential oil diffuser, inhale the scent directly from the bottle, or apply diluted oils to your pulse points.

How to Use Aromatherapy:

Step 1: Choose an essential oil that helps you feel calm (lavender is particularly popular for relaxation).

Step 2: Use a diffuser, apply a few drops to a handkerchief, or inhale directly from the bottle.

Step 3: Focus on the calming effects of the scent while practicing deep breathing. Aromatherapy can enhance relaxation and help create a sense of calm during a panic attack.

8. Stay Present and Wait It Out

Sometimes, the best thing to do during a panic attack is simply to ride it out. While this can be difficult, panic attacks are self-limiting, and they usually peak within a few minutes and then subside. Reassuring yourself that you are not in danger and that the attack will pass can help you stay grounded.

How to Wait It Out:

Step 1: Find a safe, comfortable place to sit or lie down.

Step 2: Focus on your breathing, grounding techniques, or a calming image.

Step 3: Trust that the attack will pass and that you have the strength to get through it. While this approach may require patience, it allows your body and mind to process the panic and return to a calm state.

Breathing and Relaxation Techniques: Exercises to Reduce Stress and Prevent Panic Attacks

Stress, anxiety, and panic attacks are common struggles for many, and learning how to manage these experiences is crucial for overall well-being. Breathing and relaxation techniques are some of the most effective methods to calm the nervous system, reduce stress, and prevent future panic attacks. These techniques focus on slowing down the body's natural stress response and fostering a sense of calm and control. Below are several techniques that can be helpful for reducing stress and preventing panic attacks.

1. Deep Breathing (Diaphragmatic Breathing)

Deep breathing is one of the simplest and most effective ways to combat stress and panic. It helps to activate the body's parasympathetic nervous system, which promotes relaxation and counteracts the stress response. The key to this technique is breathing deeply from the diaphragm rather than shallow chest breathing.

How to Practice Deep Breathing:

Step 1: Sit or lie down in a comfortable position. Close your eyes and relax your shoulders.

Step 2: Inhale deeply through your nose, letting your stomach rise as you fill your lungs with air. Aim for a count of 4 seconds.

Step 3: Hold your breath for 4 seconds.

Step 4: Exhale slowly and completely through your mouth for a count of 6-8 seconds.

Step 5: Repeat this for 5-10 minutes.

The goal of this technique is to breathe slowly and deeply, focusing on the rise and fall of your belly, which helps shift the body out of the "fight or flight" mode and into a more relaxed state.

2. Box Breathing

Box breathing, also known as square breathing, is a simple yet powerful technique that can help calm the nervous system. It involves inhaling, holding the breath, exhaling, and holding again, all for equal counts. This method not only helps to lower stress levels but also provides a focus to the mind, which is especially helpful during a panic attack.

How to Practice Box Breathing:
Step 1: Sit in a comfortable position with your back straight.
Step 2: Inhale slowly and deeply through your nose for a count of 4 seconds.
Step 3: Hold your breath for a count of 4 seconds.
Step 4: Exhale slowly and completely through your mouth for a count of 4 seconds.
Step 5: Hold your breath again for a count of 4 seconds.
Step 6: Repeat the cycle for several minutes, gradually increasing the count to 5 or 6 seconds if comfortable.
Box breathing is particularly useful when you're feeling overwhelmed or when you're trying to prevent a panic attack before it fully starts. It helps center your thoughts and focuses your mind on something tangible.
3. 4-7-8 Breathing
The 4-7-8 breathing technique is a popular relaxation exercise that can promote calmness and help you fall asleep more easily. This technique is known to be effective in lowering heart rate and anxiety levels. The key to this exercise is the extended exhalation phase, which is essential in signaling to your body to relax.
How to Practice 4-7-8 Breathing:
Step 1: Sit or lie down in a comfortable position.
Step 2: Close your eyes and inhale quietly through your nose for a count of 4 seconds.
Step 3: Hold your breath for a count of 7 seconds.
Step 4: Exhale completely and slowly through your mouth for a count of 8 seconds.
Step 5: Repeat this cycle 4-5 times.
This technique is a great way to regulate your breath and create a sense of calm when you're experiencing high levels of anxiety or stress.
4. Progressive Muscle Relaxation (PMR)
Progressive muscle relaxation is a technique where you intentionally tense and relax various muscle groups throughout your body. By doing this, you release tension, reduce stress, and increase overall relaxation. This method works well to counteract the muscle tension that often accompanies anxiety or panic attacks.
How to Practice Progressive Muscle Relaxation:
Step 1: Find a quiet, comfortable space where you can sit or lie down.
Step 2: Begin by taking a deep breath, then focus on one muscle group at a time (e.g., feet, legs, hands, arms, face).
Step 3: Tense the muscles in that area for 5-10 seconds, focusing on the sensation of tightness.
Step 4: Release the tension and allow the muscles to relax completely. Pay attention to how the relaxed muscles feel compared to when they were tense.
Step 5: Work your way up the body, starting from your feet and progressing to your face.
Progressive muscle relaxation helps you become more aware of where tension is stored in your body, and by releasing that tension, you allow your mind to become calmer as well.

5. Autogenic Training

Autogenic training is a relaxation technique that involves repeating calming phrases or visualizing peaceful scenarios to reduce tension and anxiety. This method focuses on creating a feeling of warmth and heaviness in your body, which helps calm both the body and the mind.

How to Practice Autogenic Training:

Step 1: Sit or lie down in a quiet, comfortable position with your eyes closed.

Step 2: Start by focusing on your breathing and letting go of any tension.

Step 3: Mentally repeat phrases such as, "My arms are heavy and warm" or "My heart is calm and steady."

Step 4: Visualize your body becoming relaxed and warm, starting from your toes and moving up toward your head.

Step 5: Practice this technique for 10-15 minutes daily to help train your body and mind to relax more easily.

Autogenic training helps to shift the body into a state of calm by focusing on specific sensations of relaxation and comfort.

6. Mindfulness Meditation

Mindfulness meditation is a form of meditation where you focus your attention on the present moment without judgment. It involves paying attention to your thoughts, feelings, and physical sensations, which helps break the cycle of stress and anxiety.

How to Practice Mindfulness Meditation:

Step 1: Sit in a comfortable position with your back straight and your hands resting on your lap or knees.

Step 2: Close your eyes and begin to focus on your breathing. Notice the sensation of the breath entering and leaving your body.

Step 3: When your mind wanders (which it naturally will), gently guide your focus back to your breath.

Step 4: If you experience anxious thoughts or feelings, acknowledge them without judgment and return to your breath.

Step 5: Practice for at least 10 minutes daily, gradually increasing the time as you become more comfortable with the practice.

Mindfulness meditation is effective for preventing panic attacks by teaching you to stay grounded in the present moment rather than getting lost in anxious thoughts or physical symptoms.

Guided Imagery or Visualization

Guided imagery or visualization is a relaxation technique where you use your imagination to create a peaceful, calming mental image or scenario. This method is especially helpful for stress reduction and can help divert your mind from anxious thoughts during a panic attack.

How to Practice Guided Imagery:

Step 1: Sit or lie in a comfortable position and close your eyes.

Step 2: Take a few deep breaths to relax.

Step 3: Picture a peaceful, relaxing scene, such as a beach, forest, or mountains. Focus on the details—what you see, hear, smell, and feel.

Step 4: Stay with the image for several minutes, allowing yourself to become fully immersed in the scene.

Step 5: Gradually bring your attention back to the present moment when you feel calm.

Guided imagery helps to take your mind away from feelings of panic and toward a more tranquil state.

Conclusion

Breathing and relaxation techniques are invaluable tools in managing stress and preventing panic attacks. Whether you use deep breathing, progressive muscle relaxation, or mindfulness meditation, these exercises can help calm your nervous system, reduce anxiety, and foster a sense of control. By practicing these techniques regularly, you can strengthen your ability to manage stress and reduce the frequency and intensity of panic attacks.

Mindfulness Therapy: How to Reduce Anxiety Through Meditation and Mindful Living

Mindfulness therapy is a powerful approach to managing anxiety, stress, and overwhelming emotions. It involves training the mind to stay present in the moment, observing thoughts, sensations, and emotions without judgment. By cultivating mindfulness, individuals can gain greater control over their anxiety and improve their emotional well-being. This approach not only helps in reducing anxiety but also promotes a greater sense of calm, clarity, and emotional resilience.

Here are several mindfulness practices and meditation techniques that can help reduce anxiety and improve overall mental health:

1. Mindful Breathing

Mindful breathing is one of the simplest and most effective mindfulness practices. By paying attention to the breath, individuals can anchor themselves in the present moment and break free from anxious thoughts.

How to Practice Mindful Breathing:

Step 1: Sit in a comfortable position with your spine straight and your hands resting on your lap.

Step 2: Close your eyes and take a deep breath in through your nose. Focus on the sensation of the air entering your nostrils and filling your lungs.

Step 3: Exhale slowly through your mouth, noticing the release of tension as you do.

Step 4: Continue to breathe naturally and pay attention to the rhythm of your breath. If your mind begins to wander, gently guide your focus back to your breath.

Step 5: Practice this for 5-10 minutes daily. Over time, it can become a natural way to calm the mind during moments of stress or anxiety.

Mindful breathing helps to regulate the body's stress response and can serve as a tool for calming the mind in any situation.

2. Body Scan Meditation
Body scan meditation is a mindfulness technique that involves scanning the body from head to toe, paying attention to any areas of tension or discomfort. This practice increases body awareness and helps to release physical tension, which can be particularly helpful during moments of anxiety.
How to Practice Body Scan Meditation:
Step 1: Lie down in a comfortable position or sit with your back straight.
Step 2: Close your eyes and take a few deep breaths to relax.
Step 3: Start at the top of your head and slowly move your attention down your body, focusing on each body part in turn (head, neck, shoulders, arms, chest, abdomen, legs, and feet).
Step 4: As you focus on each part of the body, notice any areas of tension or discomfort. Allow those areas to relax with each breath, releasing any tension.
Step 5: Continue scanning the body, making sure to focus on both physical sensations and any emotional states you may feel.
Step 6: Once you've scanned your entire body, take a few moments to notice how relaxed you feel and continue breathing deeply for a few more minutes.
This technique promotes relaxation by fostering awareness of physical sensations and helping the body release built-up tension. It's especially helpful for managing stress-induced bodily symptoms, such as muscle tightness or headaches.
3. Mindful Walking
Mindful walking is a form of moving meditation that combines mindfulness with physical activity. It can help reduce anxiety by focusing the mind on the present moment and the sensations of movement. It's also a great way to combine the benefits of exercise with relaxation.
How to Practice Mindful Walking:
Step 1: Find a quiet place to walk, whether indoors or outdoors. Begin by standing still and taking a few deep breaths.
Step 2: Start walking slowly, paying attention to each step you take. Notice how your feet lift off the ground and make contact with it.
Step 3: Focus on the sensation of walking, the movement of your legs, and how your body feels as it moves. You can also pay attention to the environment around you—what you see, hear, and feel.
Step 4: If your mind starts to wander, gently bring your focus back to the sensation of walking.
Step 5: Walk for 10-20 minutes, practicing mindfulness with each step. You can increase the duration as you become more comfortable.
Mindful walking can be especially helpful when you're feeling anxious and need to calm your mind or reduce nervous energy. The rhythm of walking can also create a sense of grounding and stability.

4. *Loving-Kindness Meditation (Metta)*

Loving-kindness meditation is a practice focused on cultivating compassion and kindness, first toward oneself and then toward others. It can help reduce anxiety by fostering a sense of connection and positivity. It is particularly helpful for those who experience self-criticism or negative thought patterns.

How to Practice Loving-Kindness Meditation:

Step 1: Sit in a comfortable position with your eyes closed. Begin by taking several deep breaths to relax.

Step 2: Start by sending loving-kindness to yourself. Mentally repeat phrases like, "May I be happy. May I be healthy. May I be at peace."

Step 3: Next, extend this loving-kindness to others. Start with someone close to you, such as a friend or family member, and repeat the phrases for them: "May you be happy. May you be healthy. May you be at peace."

Step 4: Gradually extend the loving-kindness to others in your life—acquaintances, strangers, and even those you may find difficult to interact with.

Step 5: Allow yourself to feel the warmth and compassion that arises with each repetition, noticing how it affects your mood and anxiety levels.

Loving-kindness meditation helps cultivate positive emotions and reduces the effects of anxiety by promoting a mindset of compassion, both for oneself and others.

5. *Mindful Eating*

Mindful eating involves paying full attention to the process of eating, savoring each bite, and noticing the textures, tastes, and smells of food. This practice can help reduce anxiety by bringing you into the present moment and away from anxious thoughts about the future or past.

How to Practice Mindful Eating:

Step 1: Choose a meal or snack and sit down at a table in a quiet space.

Step 2: Before eating, take a moment to appreciate the food in front of you—its colors, textures, and aromas.

Step 3: Take a small bite and chew slowly, paying attention to the taste and texture of the food. Notice the sensations in your mouth and how the food makes you feel.

Step 4: As you eat, try to stay focused on the present moment. If your mind begins to wander, gently bring your attention back to the act of eating.

Step 5: Continue to eat slowly and mindfully, savoring each bite without rushing.

Mindful eating helps improve your relationship with food, reduces overeating, and encourages a deeper connection to the present moment.

6. Mindful Journaling

Mindful journaling is a practice that involves writing about your thoughts and emotions in a non-judgmental way. By doing so, you can better understand your feelings and create space for healing and self-compassion. It also helps to externalize anxious thoughts and gain clarity on what's causing stress.

How to Practice Mindful Journaling:

Step 1: Set aside a few minutes each day to write in a quiet, comfortable space.

Step 2: Start by taking a few deep breaths to center yourself.

Step 3: Write freely about your thoughts and emotions, focusing on how you feel in the present moment. Don't worry about grammar or structure—just let your feelings flow.

Step 4: If you're feeling anxious, write about what triggered that anxiety. Explore the emotions that come up and reflect on how they may have affected your body.

Step 5: After journaling, take a few moments to read what you've written and reflect on any insights or patterns you've noticed.

Mindful journaling is a valuable tool for self-reflection and emotional regulation. It can help release pent-up emotions and provide clarity on your mental state.

Conclusion

Mindfulness therapy offers powerful tools for reducing anxiety, improving emotional regulation, and promoting overall well-being. Practices like mindful breathing, body scan meditation, and loving-kindness meditation can help shift your focus away from anxiety-provoking thoughts and bring your attention back to the present moment. By incorporating mindfulness into your daily routine, you can reduce stress, improve your emotional resilience, and cultivate a greater sense of peace and calm in your life.

Cognitive Behavioral Therapy (CBT): How to Change Thinking and Behavioral Reactions to Panic Attacks

Cognitive Behavioral Therapy (CBT) is a highly effective treatment for managing panic attacks and anxiety disorders. It is based on the principle that our thoughts, emotions, and behaviors are interconnected. By identifying and challenging negative thoughts and beliefs, and changing harmful behavioral patterns, individuals can significantly reduce the frequency and intensity of panic attacks.

CBT focuses on helping people understand the relationship between their thoughts, feelings, and actions. In the context of panic attacks, CBT teaches how distorted thinking patterns can contribute to feelings of fear and anxiety, and how altering those thoughts can change the emotional and physical responses associated with panic attacks.

Here's an overview of how CBT works to address panic attacks and help individuals regain control over their reactions:

1. Identifying and Challenging Negative Thoughts

Panic attacks are often triggered by irrational or catastrophic thinking. In CBT, one of the first steps is to identify these negative thought patterns. People with panic attacks often interpret normal physical sensations (such as increased heart rate, dizziness, or shortness of breath) as signs of a serious problem, such as a heart attack, or fear of losing control.

Steps to Identify and Challenge Negative Thoughts:

Step 1: Monitor Thoughts – Pay attention to thoughts that arise before or during a panic attack. These thoughts may include things like "I'm having a heart attack" or "I'm going to pass out."

Step 2: Identify Cognitive Distortions – These are common thinking errors, such as catastrophizing (expecting the worst outcome), overgeneralizing (seeing one event as part of a pattern), or all-or-nothing thinking (believing that things are either completely good or completely bad).

Step 3: Challenge the Thoughts – Ask yourself if the thought is realistic. For example, "Is it really likely that I am having a heart attack, or am I experiencing a panic attack?" Test the validity of the thought and look for evidence that contradicts it.

Step 4: Replace with Balanced Thoughts – After challenging negative thoughts, replace them with more balanced and realistic ones. For instance, instead of thinking "I'm going to die," think "This is uncomfortable, but it's temporary and not life-threatening."

By recognizing and reframing these distorted thoughts, individuals can reduce the fear and anxiety that often trigger panic attacks.

2. Cognitive Restructuring

Cognitive restructuring is a technique in CBT that helps individuals replace negative, irrational beliefs with healthier and more rational ones. The goal is to change the way a person interprets situations and experiences, which in turn affects their emotional and physiological responses.

How Cognitive Restructuring Works:

Step 1: Identify Beliefs About Panic Attacks – People with panic attacks often hold irrational beliefs, such as "I can't handle the physical sensations of a panic attack" or "If I have a panic attack, something terrible will happen."

Step 2: Challenge the Beliefs – Test the validity of these beliefs. For example, ask, "Have I survived previous panic attacks?" or "What evidence do I have that something catastrophic will happen?"

Step 3: Create New Beliefs – Replace irrational beliefs with more adaptive ones. For example, instead of believing "I can't cope with panic," think "Panic attacks are unpleasant, but I have the ability to manage them."

Over time, cognitive restructuring can help individuals gain confidence in their ability to cope with panic attacks and reduce the power these attacks have over them.

3. Exposure Therapy

Exposure therapy is a component of CBT that involves gradual exposure to situations or physical sensations that trigger panic. The aim is to desensitize individuals to their triggers, so they no longer provoke overwhelming fear.

How Exposure Therapy Works:

Step 1: Identify Triggers – List situations, places, or physical sensations that tend to trigger panic attacks. These could include crowded places, certain bodily sensations (like a racing heart), or specific activities (such as riding in an elevator).

Step 2: Gradual Exposure – Begin with less intimidating situations that trigger anxiety and slowly work up to more challenging scenarios. For example, if you fear your heart racing during a panic attack, practice intentionally increasing your heart rate through exercise, then focus on staying calm when your heart rate increases.

Step 3: Repeated Practice – Through repeated exposure to these triggers, you gradually learn that the feared outcomes do not occur. Over time, the anxiety associated with these triggers diminishes, and the body becomes less reactive. This exposure process helps to reduce avoidance behaviors (which reinforce panic) and encourages the individual to confront feared situations in a safe and controlled way.

4. Behavioral Activation

Behavioral activation in CBT encourages individuals to engage in activities that are rewarding and fulfilling, rather than avoiding them due to anxiety. Avoidance is a common behavior in people with panic attacks, as they may try to escape situations where they fear an attack will occur. This avoidance reinforces feelings of fear and helplessness.

How Behavioral Activation Works:

Step 1: Identify Avoidance Behaviors – These might include avoiding social events, driving, or leaving the house. Recognize which activities you have stopped doing due to fear of panic.

Step 2: Create a Gradual Plan – Set small, manageable goals for re-engaging with these activities. Start with less anxiety-provoking situations and gradually increase the difficulty level as you build confidence.

Step 3: Reward Yourself – After successfully facing a feared situation, reward yourself to reinforce the positive behavior. This can help break the cycle of avoidance and build self-confidence.

Behavioral activation can reduce feelings of isolation and helplessness, increase feelings of accomplishment, and help individuals regain control of their lives.

5. Relaxation Techniques

While CBT primarily focuses on cognitive changes, relaxation techniques are also important for managing panic attacks. These techniques can help calm the body's physical response to anxiety and reduce the intensity of a panic attack.

Common Relaxation Techniques Used in CBT:

Progressive Muscle Relaxation (PMR) – This technique involves tensing and then relaxing different muscle groups to release physical tension.

Deep Breathing – Slow, deep breathing helps activate the body's parasympathetic nervous system, which counteracts the fight-or-flight response.

Visualization – Imagining a peaceful, calm place or a relaxing activity can help shift attention away from anxiety and reduce physical symptoms of panic.

These relaxation techniques are used alongside cognitive strategies in CBT to create a comprehensive approach to managing panic attacks.

6. Mindfulness and Acceptance
Mindfulness is an important aspect of CBT for panic attacks. It involves observing your thoughts and bodily sensations without judgment or reaction. Instead of trying to control or eliminate panic symptoms, mindfulness teaches acceptance of them.
How Mindfulness Helps with Panic Attacks:
Step 1: Observe Without Judgment – When experiencing symptoms of a panic attack, practice observing the sensations (like a racing heart) without labeling them as "bad" or "scary."
Step 2: Accept the Experience – Rather than resisting the symptoms, accept them as part of the experience. Remind yourself that panic attacks are temporary and that you can cope with them.
Step 3: Focus on the Present Moment – Use grounding techniques to bring your attention back to the present moment, such as noticing what you can see, hear, and feel around you.
Mindfulness and acceptance reduce the fear of the symptoms themselves, which can prevent panic attacks from escalating and help you manage anxiety more effectively.
Conclusion
Cognitive Behavioral Therapy (CBT) is an effective treatment for panic attacks that empowers individuals to change their negative thoughts, challenge irrational beliefs, and modify their behaviors in response to fear. By using techniques such as cognitive restructuring, exposure therapy, and relaxation methods, individuals can gain better control over their panic attacks and develop healthier, more adaptive ways of coping with anxiety. CBT helps individuals to break free from the cycle of fear, allowing them to live more confidently and with greater emotional resilience.

Myths About Panic Attacks: Common Misconceptions and How They Hinder Recovery

Panic attacks are often surrounded by a cloud of misconceptions and myths that can make individuals feel misunderstood, isolated, or even reluctant to seek help. These myths not only contribute to the stigma surrounding panic attacks but can also prevent people from taking the necessary steps to manage or recover from them. Below are some of the most common myths about panic attacks and how they can hinder recovery:

1. Myth: Panic Attacks Are Just "In Your Head"

Reality: While panic attacks are heavily influenced by mental and emotional factors, they have significant physical components as well. During a panic attack, the body undergoes a series of physical changes—such as rapid heartbeat, dizziness, and shortness of breath—that are driven by the body's fight-or-flight response. These symptoms are not just imagined, but are real and often intensely distressing.

How It Hinders Recovery: The belief that panic attacks are simply a mental issue may lead individuals to dismiss the physical sensations or feel ashamed of them. This can result in avoiding medical help or not seeking treatment, leading to the worsening of symptoms over time.

2. Myth: Panic Attacks Only Happen to Weak or Anxious People

Reality: Panic attacks can affect anyone, regardless of their mental or emotional state. They are not a sign of personal weakness, nor are they a reflection of a person's inability to cope. Many people who experience panic attacks are otherwise healthy, strong, and capable individuals. Factors like stress, trauma, genetics, and even changes in brain chemistry can contribute to the development of panic attacks.

How It Hinders Recovery: The myth of weakness can make individuals feel embarrassed or ashamed of their panic attacks, leading them to hide their symptoms from others. This can increase feelings of isolation and prevent people from seeking support or treatment, which is essential for managing the condition.

3. Myth: Panic Attacks Are a Sign of a Serious Medical Condition

Reality: While the symptoms of a panic attack—such as chest pain, shortness of breath, or dizziness—can mimic those of serious medical conditions like heart attacks, panic attacks themselves are not life-threatening. The physical symptoms are caused by the body's heightened stress response, not by an underlying health problem. However, anyone experiencing these symptoms should seek medical advice to rule out other conditions.

How It Hinders Recovery: The fear that panic attacks indicate a serious medical issue can cause individuals to avoid certain situations or activities due to their concerns about health. This fear can make them more hypervigilant about their bodies, thus increasing anxiety and the likelihood of more panic attacks. Misunderstanding the benign nature of panic attacks can also delay effective treatment.

4. Myth: You Can Control a Panic Attack by Just "Calming Down"
Reality: While deep breathing and relaxation techniques can help manage the symptoms of a panic attack, the idea that you can simply "calm down" during an attack is unrealistic. Panic attacks often arise suddenly and intensely, and trying to force yourself to relax can increase feelings of frustration and helplessness. The key is to allow the attack to pass without fighting it, using coping strategies to manage the distress.
How It Hinders Recovery: Believing that you should be able to simply calm yourself down during a panic attack can lead to feelings of guilt or frustration when this doesn't happen. This can increase anxiety and perpetuate a cycle of self-blame, making it harder to find effective coping mechanisms and prolonging the attack.
5. Myth: If You Have Panic Attacks, You're Destined to Have Them Forever
Reality: Panic attacks are treatable, and many individuals who experience them can learn to manage or even eliminate their symptoms through treatment and coping strategies. Cognitive Behavioral Therapy (CBT), exposure therapy, medication, and relaxation techniques are all effective methods for reducing the frequency and intensity of panic attacks. With the right support, it is entirely possible to regain control over your life and your body's response to stress.
How It Hinders Recovery: The belief that panic attacks are permanent can lead to hopelessness and a sense of helplessness. This mindset can prevent individuals from seeking help or trying new strategies, reinforcing the cycle of panic and anxiety. It can also lead to avoidance behaviors, such as avoiding social situations, that only reinforce the fear of having another attack.
6. Myth: Panic Attacks Only Occur in Certain Places or Situations
Reality: While certain situations may trigger panic attacks, they can occur in any setting, even in places or activities that have previously felt safe. Panic attacks are often unpredictable, and the triggers can vary from person to person. The fear of having an attack in a specific situation, like a crowded space or during a meeting, can itself become a trigger, making the person more likely to experience an attack in that environment.
How It Hinders Recovery: Believing that panic attacks are confined to specific situations can lead to avoidance behavior, where individuals limit their activities or stay away from certain places for fear of having an attack. This can severely restrict their lifestyle and prevent them from leading a full, unrestricted life.

7. Myth: Panic Attacks Are a Form of Attention-Seeking

Reality: Panic attacks are not a way for people to seek attention or sympathy. They are a distressing and uncontrollable experience that happens in response to internal triggers, often with no outward cause. While it's natural to seek support during difficult moments, the symptoms of a panic attack are not deliberate or exaggerated.

How It Hinders Recovery: This myth can contribute to feelings of shame and guilt, causing individuals to hide their symptoms or avoid discussing them with others. It can also result in unsupportive reactions from family or friends, who might dismiss the severity of the experience or misunderstand its nature. Lack of understanding and support can make it harder for individuals to seek help and recovery.

8. Myth: People Who Experience Panic Attacks Are Mentally Ill

Reality: Panic attacks are a symptom of anxiety disorders, but they do not necessarily mean someone is mentally ill. Many people experience panic attacks as a result of stress, trauma, or even genetics. These attacks are treatable, and experiencing them does not indicate a lifelong mental illness. Mental health conditions such as generalized anxiety disorder or panic disorder may contribute to panic attacks, but they are not the sole cause.

How It Hinders Recovery: Labeling panic attacks as a sign of mental illness can prevent people from seeking help, as they may fear being judged or labeled. It can also lead to stigma, which discourages open discussions about mental health and limits access to resources for recovery.

9. Myth: Medications Are the Only Way to Treat Panic Attacks

Reality: While medication can be an effective part of treatment for some people, it is not the only option. Therapy, particularly Cognitive Behavioral Therapy (CBT), and self-help techniques such as mindfulness, breathing exercises, and lifestyle changes can also be very effective in managing panic attacks. Many people find that a combination of approaches, including therapy and medication, works best for them.

How It Hinders Recovery: The belief that medication is the only solution can lead individuals to rely solely on pills, potentially neglecting other valuable treatment options. It can also make them feel that recovery is out of their control or dependent on pharmaceutical interventions.

Conclusion

Understanding and debunking myths about panic attacks is a crucial step in the recovery process. The misconceptions surrounding panic attacks can exacerbate anxiety, reinforce feelings of shame, and prevent people from seeking the help and support they need. By recognizing the reality of panic attacks and challenging these myths, individuals can take the necessary steps toward healing, regain control over their symptoms, and live a more fulfilling life.

Pharmaceutical Approaches: When It's Necessary

An Overview of Medication and Its Effectiveness

While many individuals can manage panic attacks through therapy and coping strategies, some may find that medication plays an essential role in their recovery process. Medications can be particularly useful for those who experience frequent or severe panic attacks that significantly impact their daily life. In this section, we will explore the role of medication in treating panic attacks, when it is necessary, and how effective it can be.

1. Types of Medications for Panic Attacks

There are several classes of medications commonly used to treat panic attacks, each with its specific benefits and side effects:

a. Antidepressants (SSRIs and SNRIs)

Selective serotonin reuptake inhibitors (SSRIs) and serotonin-norepinephrine reuptake inhibitors (SNRIs) are commonly prescribed for panic disorder and other anxiety-related conditions. These medications help to regulate serotonin and norepinephrine levels in the brain, which can improve mood and reduce anxiety symptoms.

Common SSRIs and SNRIs include:

Fluoxetine (Prozac)

Sertraline (Zoloft)

Escitalopram (Lexapro)

Venlafaxine (Effexor)

Effectiveness: SSRIs and SNRIs are generally considered first-line treatments for panic disorder. They are effective for long-term management, helping to reduce the frequency and intensity of panic attacks over time.

Side Effects: Common side effects may include nausea, insomnia, fatigue, and sexual dysfunction. These effects often diminish as the body adjusts to the medication.

b. Benzodiazepines

Benzodiazepines are fast-acting medications that can provide immediate relief from panic attacks. They work by depressing the central nervous system, which reduces symptoms of anxiety and panic.

Common benzodiazepines include:

Alprazolam (Xanax)

Lorazepam (Ativan)

Clonazepam (Klonopin)

Effectiveness: Benzodiazepines are highly effective in reducing the acute symptoms of panic attacks. However, they are typically prescribed for short-term use due to the risk of dependence and tolerance.

Side Effects: Side effects may include drowsiness, dizziness, confusion, and coordination problems. Long-term use can lead to dependence and withdrawal symptoms if the medication is stopped abruptly.

c. Beta-Blockers

Beta-blockers, such as propranolol, are sometimes prescribed to help manage the physical symptoms of anxiety, such as rapid heart rate, trembling, and shaking, that occur during a panic attack.

Effectiveness: Beta-blockers do not directly address the underlying psychological symptoms of panic attacks but can help control the physical manifestations, making them useful in situations where anxiety or panic attacks are triggered by a specific event, such as public speaking.

Side Effects: Common side effects include dizziness, fatigue, and cold extremities. Beta-blockers are generally well-tolerated but should be used with caution in individuals with certain heart conditions.

d. Antipsychotics (in some cases)

In some cases, atypical antipsychotic medications may be prescribed to treat panic disorder, especially when it co-occurs with other conditions such as depression or severe anxiety disorders.

Effectiveness: Antipsychotics are usually considered when other treatments have not been effective. They may help manage severe anxiety and agitation, but they are generally not the first-line treatment for panic attacks.

Side Effects: Potential side effects include weight gain, drowsiness, and metabolic changes. These medications should be monitored closely by a healthcare provider.

2. When Is Medication Necessary?

Medication may be necessary in the following cases:

a. Severe or Frequent Panic Attacks

If panic attacks occur regularly or are particularly severe, medication can help reduce the intensity and frequency, providing relief while other treatment methods (like therapy) are being implemented.

b. Interference with Daily Life

For individuals whose panic attacks significantly interfere with their ability to function, such as avoiding work, school, or social situations, medication can be an important tool for stabilizing symptoms.

c. Co-occurring Disorders

When panic disorder is accompanied by other mental health conditions, such as depression, generalized anxiety disorder, or PTSD, medication may be prescribed to address the broader spectrum of symptoms and improve overall mental health.

d. Short-Term Management

Some people may need medication on a short-term basis during particularly stressful or triggering periods (e.g., before a big event or during a significant life change) to help manage anxiety until the underlying issues can be addressed through therapy.

3. Effectiveness of Medication
While medication can be highly effective for many individuals, it is typically most beneficial when combined with other treatments, such as psychotherapy. Research has shown that Cognitive Behavioral Therapy (CBT), in particular, is an effective method for treating panic disorder and can help individuals learn how to manage their anxiety without relying solely on medication.
For some individuals, medication alone may not be sufficient to manage panic attacks, as it does not address the root causes of anxiety. Therefore, a comprehensive treatment plan that includes therapy, lifestyle changes, and coping strategies is often recommended for the best long-term results.
4. Potential Risks and Considerations
While medication can be a valuable tool in managing panic attacks, it is not without risks. Some important considerations include:
Dependence and Tolerance: Certain medications, such as benzodiazepines, carry the risk of physical dependence and tolerance, meaning that higher doses may be needed over time to achieve the same effect.
Side Effects: All medications come with potential side effects, which can range from mild to severe. It's essential for individuals to work closely with their healthcare provider to find the right medication and dosage to minimize side effects.
Long-Term Use: For many individuals, medication is most effective when used for a specific period while they are also working on managing their symptoms through other methods, such as therapy or self-help techniques. Prolonged reliance on medication without addressing underlying causes may limit overall recovery.
5. Conclusion
Medication can be a crucial part of the treatment plan for individuals experiencing frequent or severe panic attacks. When used appropriately, it can help alleviate symptoms, stabilize mood, and improve overall functioning. However, it is important to recognize that medication is not a cure in itself. A holistic approach that includes therapy, lifestyle changes, and coping strategies is often the most effective way to manage panic attacks and improve quality of life. Always consult with a healthcare provider to determine the best course of treatment based on individual needs and circumstances.

Social Aspects: The Impact of Panic Attacks on Life

How Panic Attacks Affect Relationships and Career

Panic attacks are not just a personal challenge; they can also have far-reaching consequences on various aspects of an individual's life, especially in terms of social relationships and career. The emotional, physical, and psychological toll of frequent panic attacks often extends beyond the individual, influencing interactions with family, friends, coworkers, and even employers. Understanding these social aspects is crucial for those struggling with panic attacks, as well as for the people in their lives, so that they can navigate the impact more effectively.

1. Impact on Relationships

a. Strained Family Dynamics

Panic attacks can place a significant strain on family relationships, especially when they occur frequently. Family members may feel helpless or frustrated because they don't know how to support their loved one during an attack. They may also experience anxiety themselves, as they worry about the person having another panic attack.

Common challenges include:

Misunderstanding: Family members may not fully understand panic attacks and might dismiss them as overreaction or attention-seeking behavior.

Increased caregiving: Individuals who suffer from panic attacks may need constant reassurance, which can put a burden on their family members.

Avoidance: As panic attacks lead to avoidance of certain situations or places, families might struggle with disrupted plans, missed events, or social isolation.

b. Impact on Romantic Relationships

In romantic relationships, panic attacks can lead to feelings of frustration, helplessness, or confusion for both partners. The partner with panic disorder may feel guilty or embarrassed about their reactions, which can affect their self-esteem and emotional connection. The other partner may feel burdened or overwhelmed by the responsibility of providing support during an attack.

Challenges for couples include:

Miscommunication: If one partner does not understand panic attacks, they may not provide the right kind of support, causing tension in the relationship.

Emotional exhaustion: Constantly being in a state of high alert, due to the unpredictability of panic attacks, can lead to emotional fatigue and burnout for both partners.

Increased dependency: The person experiencing panic attacks may become overly reliant on their partner for comfort and reassurance, which can disrupt the balance of the relationship.

c. Friendships and Social Life
Panic attacks can also affect friendships and a person's social life. People with panic disorder may begin to withdraw from social activities due to the fear of experiencing an attack in public or in front of others. This withdrawal can lead to isolation, which exacerbates feelings of loneliness and anxiety.
Social challenges include:
Avoiding social gatherings: Fear of a panic attack at a social event can lead to avoiding gatherings, which might lead to strained friendships or misunderstandings.
Difficulty explaining the disorder: Some people may find it hard to explain what a panic attack feels like, which can result in friends misunderstanding the condition and possibly distancing themselves.
Stigma: There is often a stigma surrounding mental health, including panic disorder. This stigma can make it even more difficult for someone to seek help or confide in others, which further isolates them from their social network.
2. Impact on Career
a. Job Performance and Productivity
Panic attacks can have a significant impact on work performance. The fear of experiencing a panic attack in the workplace, especially in stressful or public situations, can lead to avoidance of certain tasks or responsibilities. This avoidance can result in decreased productivity and may impact career advancement or opportunities.
Challenges at work include:
Reduced focus and concentration: Frequent panic attacks can make it difficult for individuals to stay focused on tasks, leading to mistakes or missed deadlines.
Avoidance of certain work situations: Employees might avoid presentations, meetings, or other situations that could trigger a panic attack, which can limit their professional opportunities.
Increased absenteeism: Individuals may call in sick or take frequent mental health days due to the fear of a panic attack occurring at work, leading to reduced attendance.
b. Workplace Relationships
Panic attacks can also affect interactions with colleagues and supervisors. If coworkers or managers are unaware of the condition, they may interpret the individual's behavior as being unprofessional, unreliable, or disengaged. This can strain workplace relationships and even harm an individual's reputation within the organization.
Challenges with colleagues include:
Misunderstanding: If coworkers don't understand the nature of panic attacks, they may view the individual as difficult to work with, potentially leading to a lack of support from the team.
Judgment: In some cases, individuals with panic disorder may be judged negatively by coworkers or supervisors, which can affect their professional image and opportunities for promotion.
Discrimination: In extreme cases, panic disorder can lead to workplace discrimination, as employers may be concerned about the individual's ability to perform under pressure or handle stressful situations.

c. Fear of Losing Employment

The fear of experiencing a panic attack at work can cause significant anxiety for individuals with panic disorder. The stress of trying to maintain composure while also fearing an attack can lead to burnout and an increased risk of quitting a job, even when it is not necessarily the best decision for their career. Concerns about job security include:

Lack of understanding from employers: Many employers are still not well-versed in mental health issues, and may not provide reasonable accommodations for individuals suffering from panic disorder. This can make it harder for the person to remain in the workforce.

Fear of being judged: Individuals may worry that their condition will affect how they are perceived by their employer or coworkers, making them hesitant to ask for accommodations or support.

3. Coping Strategies for Managing Social and Career Impact

a. Open Communication

Being open about one's condition with trusted family members, friends, or coworkers can help reduce misunderstandings and build a supportive environment. While it may be difficult to discuss, providing some education about panic disorder can help others understand and offer the necessary support.

b. Seeking Professional Help

Therapy, such as Cognitive Behavioral Therapy (CBT), can help individuals learn how to manage their panic attacks, reducing their impact on relationships and career. CBT focuses on changing thought patterns and behaviors that contribute to panic attacks, improving coping skills in social and professional environments.

c. Building a Support Network

Having a reliable support network is essential for managing panic attacks. This can include a combination of family, friends, mental health professionals, and even support groups. Knowing that there are people who understand and offer support can alleviate feelings of isolation.

d. Workplace Adjustments

For those whose careers are affected by panic attacks, it may be beneficial to discuss reasonable accommodations with employers. Flexible work hours, the option to work from home, or permission to take breaks when feeling anxious can help reduce work-related stress and improve job performance.

4. Conclusion

Panic attacks can profoundly impact social relationships and careers, often creating challenges in communication, understanding, and productivity. However, with proper support, understanding, and treatment, individuals can manage their panic attacks more effectively and mitigate the negative effects on their personal and professional lives. Open dialogue, professional help, and coping strategies are key to reducing the social and career impact of panic attacks and helping individuals live fulfilling, successful lives despite the challenges they face.

Isolation and Shame: The Emotional Side of Panic

How to Deal with Feelings of Loneliness and Shame

Panic attacks are not only physically overwhelming but also emotionally draining. Alongside the fear and physical symptoms, individuals often experience deep feelings of isolation and shame. These emotions can exacerbate the struggle with panic disorder, creating a cycle of withdrawal and emotional distress. Understanding how isolation and shame contribute to the experience of panic and how to manage them is essential in the healing process.

1. Isolation: The Loneliness of Panic

Panic attacks can lead individuals to withdraw from social situations, leading to isolation. The fear of having a panic attack in public or around others can cause a person to avoid gatherings, events, or even casual outings. Over time, this avoidance behavior may create a sense of disconnection from others, making the person feel increasingly isolated and alone.

a. Avoidance of Social Situations

The fear of having a panic attack in front of others is a common concern. People may feel ashamed or embarrassed by the idea of having a visible panic attack, which could lead them to avoid situations where they might feel vulnerable. This can include:

Avoiding parties, gatherings, or events.

Skipping work or social engagements to prevent the possibility of an attack.

Withdrawing from friends or family members who don't understand the condition.

b. Self-imposed Isolation

As the panic attacks continue, the person might start to isolate themselves more intentionally. They may believe that their condition is too difficult for others to understand, which leads to a sense of being different or "broken." Over time, this isolation becomes self-perpetuating, as the individual may feel increasingly disconnected from the world around them. This can result in:

Distancing from relationships due to the fear of burdening others.

Avoiding therapy or professional help out of fear of being judged.

A growing sense of loneliness as they choose to stay home or limit their interactions.

c. The Impact on Mental Health

The isolation that comes with panic attacks can worsen the condition. Loneliness and isolation are linked to increased anxiety, depression, and other mental health issues. Being cut off from social support and avoiding professional help can create a downward spiral, where the individual feels trapped in their own mind, unable to escape the cycle of panic, fear, and solitude.

2. Shame: The Emotional Weight of Panic

Shame is a powerful emotion that often accompanies panic attacks. Many people with panic disorder feel embarrassed by their symptoms, believing they are weak or incapable of controlling their emotions. This internalized shame can lead to feelings of inadequacy and self-blame, which may prevent them from seeking help or talking about their experiences.

a. Fear of Being Judged

Shame is often rooted in the fear of being judged by others. Individuals with panic attacks may worry that people will see them as irrational, overly sensitive, or unstable. This fear can prevent them from sharing their experiences with friends or family, leading to emotional isolation. Common fears include:

Being labeled as weak: Many individuals feel ashamed that they are unable to control their anxiety, believing that others may see them as lacking strength.

Appearing out of control: Panic attacks can be very intense, and the loss of control during an attack can heighten feelings of embarrassment or shame.

Burdening others: People with panic attacks may worry that they are being a burden to their loved ones, especially if the attacks occur frequently or disrupt plans.

b. Internalized Stigma

The shame associated with panic attacks is often internalized, meaning the individual believes they are fundamentally flawed because of their condition. This self-stigma can prevent them from reaching out for support, as they may feel unworthy of help. It can also result in:

Self-criticism: A person might harshly judge themselves for experiencing panic, further increasing their anxiety and emotional pain.

Denial: Some individuals may try to ignore or suppress their symptoms, hoping they will go away, but this only makes the feelings of shame stronger.

Self-isolation: Because of this stigma, the person may avoid seeking treatment, socializing, or even acknowledging the severity of their condition.

c. Cultural and Societal Factors

Cultural attitudes toward mental health can contribute to feelings of shame. In many societies, there is still a stigma around mental illness, including panic disorder. People may feel they are not living up to societal expectations of being calm, composed, or "normal." This societal pressure can:

Perpetuate the idea that panic attacks are a sign of weakness or failure.

Discourage individuals from seeking professional help, out of fear of being labeled as mentally unstable.

Increase the emotional burden of panic attacks, as individuals internalize these societal beliefs and feel inadequate for struggling with their mental health.

3. Managing Isolation and Shame
a. Opening Up to Trusted People
One of the first steps in dealing with isolation and shame is to open up to trusted individuals. Sharing the experience of panic attacks can reduce the emotional weight and help others understand what is happening. Trusted family members, friends, or therapists can offer empathy and support, which can break the cycle of isolation.
How to do this:
Choose someone who is understanding and compassionate, and who is open to learning about panic attacks.
Explain the condition in a way that helps them understand your feelings and symptoms.
Reassure them that it is not their fault and that you are working on managing the attacks.
b. Seeking Professional Help
Therapy, especially Cognitive Behavioral Therapy (CBT), is an effective way to combat both the shame and isolation associated with panic attacks. CBT helps individuals understand their thought patterns and behaviors, allowing them to reframe negative beliefs about themselves and their condition. A therapist can also help the individual develop coping mechanisms to reduce the emotional impact of panic attacks.
Benefits of therapy include:
Learning to challenge negative thoughts and beliefs about oneself.
Developing strategies to manage anxiety and panic in social or work situations.
Gaining confidence in talking about panic attacks without feeling ashamed.
c. Building a Support Network
Having a support network of individuals who understand and accept your condition is crucial. This can include family, friends, support groups, or online communities where people with similar experiences can share advice and encouragement. Being part of a support network can alleviate feelings of loneliness and provide validation.
How to build a support network:
Join a support group, either in person or online, for people with anxiety or panic disorders.
Seek out online forums where others can share their experiences and provide support.
Reach out to loved ones and let them know how they can best support you.
d. Practice Self-compassion
Shame can be alleviated by practicing self-compassion. Understanding that panic attacks are a medical condition, not a reflection of personal failure, can help reduce self-criticism. Being kind to oneself, acknowledging the courage it takes to face panic attacks, and celebrating small victories can help break the cycle of shame.
Ways to practice self-compassion:
Avoid harsh self-talk and replace it with more supportive, understanding thoughts.
Recognize that panic attacks are not a reflection of personal weakness, but rather an emotional response to stress.
Acknowledge the progress you have made in managing panic attacks, no matter how small.

The Power of Support: Working with Loved Ones

How Friends and Family Can Help in the Fight Against Panic

When dealing with panic attacks, having a strong support system can make a significant difference. While therapy and self-help strategies are crucial in managing the condition, the support of friends and family can offer essential emotional comfort, encouragement, and practical help during moments of distress. Understanding how loved ones can assist in the recovery process can empower both the individual experiencing panic attacks and those around them.

1. Understanding Panic Attacks: The First Step for Loved Ones

Before offering support, it is essential that friends and family understand what panic attacks are and how they manifest. Panic attacks are sudden and intense episodes of fear and anxiety that often occur without warning. The person experiencing a panic attack may feel a racing heart, difficulty breathing, dizziness, and a strong sense of impending doom. These symptoms can be terrifying, both for the individual and for those witnessing the attack.

a. Educating Yourself

Loved ones should educate themselves about panic attacks and anxiety disorders. Understanding that panic attacks are not a sign of weakness or irrationality, but a medical condition, can help reduce feelings of frustration or confusion. It also allows them to offer more empathetic and effective support. Resources such as books, articles, and videos from mental health professionals can provide valuable insight into how to best support someone dealing with panic.

b. Empathy and Patience

Being empathetic and patient is crucial when supporting someone with panic attacks. Recognizing that these experiences are genuinely distressing and not something the person can control can foster compassion. Understanding that it's not about being "strong enough" to stop the attack, but rather managing the symptoms, can help friends and family respond more appropriately.

2. Practical Support During a Panic Attack

Knowing what to do during an actual panic attack can help the individual feel more supported and less alone in the moment. Loved ones can provide practical strategies that help the person manage their symptoms and regain a sense of control.

a. Stay Calm and Reassuring

One of the most important things a friend or family member can do is remain calm. The individual experiencing a panic attack may feel overwhelmed and out of control, and the presence of a calm, reassuring figure can be comforting. Offering words of reassurance like, "You're safe," or "This will pass," can help the person feel grounded. It's essential to avoid showing panic or distress yourself, as it can escalate the situation.

b. Encourage Breathing Exercises

Panic attacks often cause rapid, shallow breathing, which can make the individual feel even more anxious. Helping the person focus on deep breathing can calm the nervous system. Encourage slow, deep breaths by saying, "Breathe in deeply for four counts, hold, and exhale slowly for four counts." Breathing exercises can help slow the heart rate and provide the individual with a sense of control.

c. Create a Safe Environment

During a panic attack, the individual may feel trapped or unable to escape the overwhelming feelings of fear. It's important to help them feel safe and secure. This can be achieved by:

Finding a quiet, private space away from distractions or crowds.
Offering a comforting touch, such as holding their hand (if they're comfortable with it).
Ensuring that they have enough space to breathe and not feel physically constrained.

d. Avoid Dismissing Their Experience

It's crucial not to downplay the severity of the panic attack by saying things like, "It's just in your head," or "You're overreacting." These kinds of statements can invalidate the person's experience and increase feelings of shame or embarrassment. Instead, acknowledging the difficulty of the situation by saying something like, "I know this feels really scary right now," helps the person feel understood.

3. Providing Emotional Support and Encouragement
Beyond the immediate moment of a panic attack, emotional support from loved
ones is key to long-term healing. Building a supportive, understanding environment
at home can help reduce the frequency and intensity of panic attacks.
a. Listen Without Judging
Being a non-judgmental listener is one of the most important things friends and
family can do. Sometimes, the person experiencing panic attacks simply needs to
talk about their feelings and fears. Listening actively and without interruption,
offering validation for their feelings, and avoiding any form of criticism can create a
safe space for them to express themselves.
b. Encourage Treatment and Professional Help
While friends and family members can provide great emotional support, they are not
trained to treat panic attacks. Encouraging the individual to seek professional help
from a therapist or mental health specialist is important. Many people with panic
attacks benefit from Cognitive Behavioral Therapy (CBT), which helps them
understand their thought patterns and learn coping mechanisms for managing their
symptoms.
c. Offer Practical Help with Daily Activities
For some individuals, panic attacks can affect their ability to perform everyday tasks.
Friends and family can assist by offering to help with activities that may seem
overwhelming during periods of anxiety. This could include:
Helping with household chores, grocery shopping, or running errands.
Offering emotional support during challenging situations (e.g., going to a doctor's
appointment or social event).
Being available for check-ins and encouragement throughout the day.
d. Reassure and Celebrate Small Wins
Panic attacks can often leave the individual feeling defeated or discouraged.
Reassurance that progress is being made can be invaluable. Celebrating small
victories, like managing to leave the house or participate in a social event, can help
boost confidence and motivation. Let the person know that overcoming panic
attacks is a process and that every step forward counts.

4. Establishing Healthy Boundaries
While supporting someone with panic attacks is important, it's also essential for loved ones to establish healthy boundaries. Supporting someone with a mental health condition can be emotionally taxing, and it's crucial that friends and family members take care of their own well-being too.

a. Set Realistic Expectations
Understand that there will be ups and downs in the recovery process. Recovery from panic attacks doesn't happen overnight, and there will be periods of improvement as well as setbacks. It's important to manage expectations and recognize that the individual may need time, patience, and support to heal fully.

b. Practice Self-care
Supporting someone through panic attacks can be demanding. It's important for friends and family to take care of their own mental health by practicing self-care. This can involve taking time for themselves, engaging in activities that relax and restore their energy, and seeking support if they find the situation emotionally overwhelming.

c. Seek Outside Support
If the strain of supporting someone with panic attacks becomes too much, loved ones should seek outside support as well. This could be in the form of therapy, support groups for families of individuals with anxiety disorders, or counseling services that offer guidance on how to cope with the challenges of supporting a loved one.

5. Conclusion
The role of friends and family in the fight against panic attacks is indispensable. With empathy, education, and practical support, loved ones can provide comfort and stability during difficult times. Encouraging treatment, practicing patience, and creating an emotionally supportive environment can make a significant difference in the person's journey toward healing. However, it's equally important for loved ones to take care of their own emotional needs and seek help when needed, ensuring they can continue to offer meaningful support without neglecting their own well-being.

Life After Attacks: The Path to Recovery

How to Rebuild Confidence and Plan for the Future

Experiencing panic attacks can significantly disrupt your life, leaving you feeling overwhelmed, out of control, and uncertain about the future. However, the journey toward recovery is not only possible but can also lead to a renewed sense of strength, resilience, and hope. Life after panic attacks involves rebuilding confidence, regaining control over your mental and emotional well-being, and developing a positive outlook on what lies ahead.

1. Understanding the Recovery Process

The process of recovery from panic attacks is unique to each individual, but it often involves several stages of healing. Recognizing that this is a gradual journey and allowing yourself the space and time to heal is crucial. It's important to approach recovery with compassion, acknowledging that setbacks may occur, but they do not define your progress.

a. Acceptance and Self-Compassion

The first step in recovery is accepting that panic attacks are part of your experience, but they do not have to define you. It's essential to be compassionate toward yourself and recognize that healing is a process. Self-compassion involves treating yourself with the same care and understanding you would offer a close friend in a similar situation.

b. Acknowledging Your Strength

Even though panic attacks can make you feel vulnerable, they also offer opportunities for growth. Acknowledge the strength it has taken to face these challenges. Recognizing the courage in continuing to live your life despite these attacks can help shift your focus toward resilience rather than fear.

2. Regaining Confidence

Confidence is often shaken after a series of panic attacks, especially when you feel like you cannot trust your body or your mind. Regaining confidence involves taking small steps toward re-engaging with life and proving to yourself that you can handle difficult situations.

a. Facing Fears Gradually

One effective method of rebuilding confidence is gradually facing the situations that trigger your panic attacks. This process, known as exposure therapy, involves confronting feared situations in a controlled and manageable way, allowing you to slowly build tolerance and reduce the intensity of your anxiety. For example, if crowds cause you anxiety, start by spending short amounts of time in less crowded places and gradually increase exposure as you feel comfortable.

b. Setting Achievable Goals

Rebuilding confidence also involves setting small, achievable goals that will help you feel a sense of accomplishment. These goals can range from daily activities, such as leaving the house for a walk, to larger challenges, like returning to work or socializing with friends. Achieving these goals, no matter how small, will gradually help rebuild your sense of self-efficacy.

c. Celebrating Progress

It's important to celebrate each step forward, no matter how minor it may seem. Recognizing your progress allows you to acknowledge your strength and resilience, boosting your confidence and motivation. Whether it's simply making it through the day without a panic attack or handling a stressful situation more calmly, take time to celebrate your achievements.

3. Building a New Outlook on Life

As you recover from panic attacks, you may find that your perspective on life changes. This transformation can offer new opportunities for growth, self-discovery, and even fulfillment. Rebuilding your future after panic attacks involves redefining what you want out of life and setting new, empowering goals.

a. Reassessing Priorities

The experience of dealing with panic attacks can lead to a shift in your values and priorities. You may find that certain things that once felt important—such as work pressure, social expectations, or material pursuits—are no longer as significant. This shift can help you focus on what truly matters to you, such as relationships, personal growth, or creative fulfillment.

b. Developing New Coping Skills

A major part of recovery is developing new coping mechanisms for managing anxiety and stress. These skills can range from mindfulness and relaxation techniques to physical activities, hobbies, or journaling. Developing a toolkit of strategies that work for you will help you navigate future stressors with greater ease, reinforcing your sense of control and self-efficacy.

c. Setting Long-Term Goals

Looking to the future, setting long-term goals can help provide direction and purpose. These goals might involve improving mental health, exploring new career paths, or building more meaningful relationships. Focus on what excites you and inspires you, and break down these larger goals into manageable steps. This will give you something positive to work toward and help you stay motivated during your recovery journey.

4. Seeking Ongoing Support
Even as you regain confidence and move forward, it's important to continue seeking support from friends, family, and mental health professionals. Recovery doesn't mean doing everything alone—having a support system can provide you with encouragement, guidance, and a sense of community.
a. Therapy and Counseling
While you may feel better after a period of recovery, therapy can continue to be a helpful resource for maintaining progress. Therapies such as Cognitive Behavioral Therapy (CBT) or Acceptance and Commitment Therapy (ACT) can help you develop lasting skills for managing anxiety and preventing panic attacks in the future.
b. Support Groups
Support groups, whether in-person or online, can offer a sense of connection with others who understand what you're going through. Sharing experiences, challenges, and successes with others who have faced similar struggles can provide comfort and reduce feelings of isolation.
c. Maintaining Healthy Relationships
Strong, supportive relationships with loved ones can help bolster your recovery. Surrounding yourself with people who understand your struggles and encourage your growth can keep you motivated and offer emotional stability. At the same time, be mindful of setting boundaries with people who may not be supportive or understanding of your experiences.
5. Embracing a New Chapter
Life after panic attacks is not about returning to the way things were before but rather embracing a new chapter in your life. It's about rebuilding your self-worth, regaining confidence, and developing a healthier relationship with your mind and body. The path to recovery may be winding, but every step forward brings you closer to a life that feels fulfilling, purposeful, and manageable.
By focusing on healing, embracing self-compassion, and setting meaningful goals for the future, you can rebuild your life after panic attacks. While the journey may be long, with the right strategies, support, and mindset, you can emerge stronger and more confident, ready to face whatever comes your way.

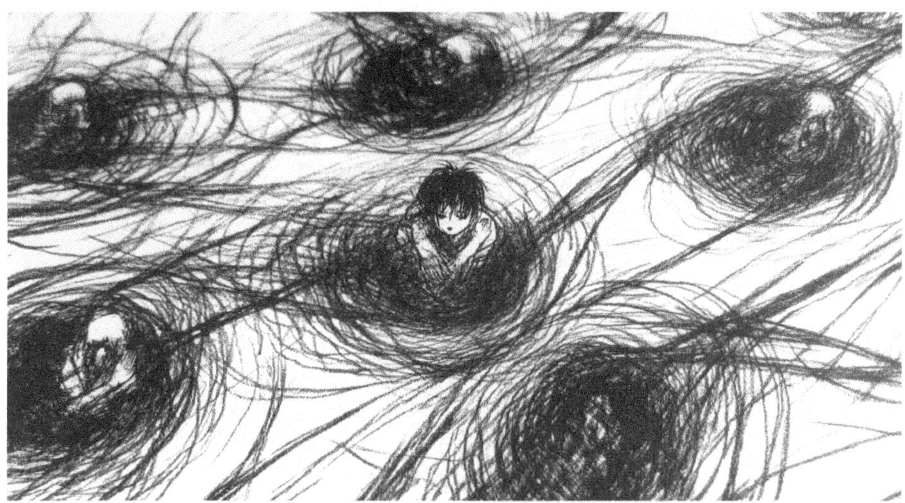

1. Recognizing Early Warning Signs

One of the key strategies in preventing recurring panic attacks is to become aware of the early warning signs that may indicate a potential episode. These early signs can include subtle changes in physical sensations, emotions, or thoughts, which can signal that stress or anxiety is building up.

a. Physical Sensations

Before a panic attack, some people experience physical signs such as shallow breathing, a racing heartbeat, or tightness in the chest. Becoming more attuned to your body's signals can help you take action before a full-blown panic attack occurs.

b. Negative Thought Patterns

Thoughts of impending doom, fear of losing control, or catastrophic thinking can also signal that anxiety is rising. Identifying these thought patterns early allows you to challenge them before they escalate.

c. Emotional Awareness

Recognizing when you're feeling particularly stressed, anxious, or overwhelmed can help you address your emotional state before it leads to a panic attack. Taking note of your emotional triggers and responses can empower you to manage your stress levels more effectively.

2. Developing Healthy Coping Mechanisms

Having effective coping strategies in place can significantly reduce the likelihood of panic attacks. Coping mechanisms help you manage stress and anxiety in a healthy way, preventing it from overwhelming you.

a. Mindfulness and Meditation

Practices such as mindfulness meditation, deep breathing, or progressive muscle relaxation can be extremely effective in managing anxiety. These techniques help you stay grounded in the present moment and prevent runaway thoughts that could lead to panic. By regularly practicing mindfulness, you train your mind to stay calm and focused, even during stressful situations.

b. Physical Activity

Exercise is one of the most powerful tools for preventing panic attacks. Regular physical activity helps reduce stress hormones, increase endorphins, and improve overall mental health. Whether it's a walk in nature, yoga, or more intense exercise, physical activity can help you stay resilient and balanced.

c. Journaling and Reflection

Writing down your thoughts and emotions can help you process stress and identify patterns that lead to anxiety. Journaling allows you to reflect on your day, identify stressors, and track your progress in managing your emotions. This practice also creates space to focus on the positive, reinforcing a sense of control over your emotional state.

3. Maintaining a Balanced Lifestyle

A balanced lifestyle is crucial in supporting your emotional health and preventing future panic attacks. Taking care of your body, mind, and relationships helps build a strong foundation for resilience.

a. Sleep Hygiene

Poor sleep can significantly impact your emotional well-being and increase the risk of panic attacks. Maintaining a regular sleep schedule, creating a relaxing bedtime routine, and prioritizing restful sleep can help keep your body and mind in balance.

b. Nutrition

What you eat has a direct impact on your emotional health. A balanced diet rich in whole foods, including vegetables, fruits, and healthy fats, can help stabilize your mood and energy levels. Limiting caffeine, sugar, and alcohol can also reduce anxiety and prevent panic attacks.

c. Time for Relaxation and Enjoyment

Engage in activities that bring you joy and relaxation. Whether it's reading, listening to music, spending time with loved ones, or pursuing a hobby, incorporating relaxation into your routine can help prevent burnout and stress accumulation. Taking breaks and allowing yourself to recharge is essential for long-term emotional well-being.

4. Building Emotional Resilience

Building resilience is essential in protecting yourself from recurring panic attacks. Resilience involves developing the ability to bounce back from challenges and maintaining a positive mindset even in difficult situations.

a. Cognitive Behavioral Strategies

Cognitive Behavioral Therapy (CBT) is a powerful tool in preventing panic attacks. CBT helps you identify and challenge negative thought patterns, replacing them with more realistic and constructive ones. By practicing these strategies regularly, you train your brain to respond to stressors in a more balanced and less anxiety-provoking way.

b. Developing Positive Self-Talk

How you talk to yourself has a significant impact on your emotional state. Replacing negative or catastrophic thoughts with positive affirmations can help reduce anxiety and prevent panic attacks. Remind yourself of your strength, resilience, and ability to handle challenges as they come.

c. Seeking Support

Surrounding yourself with a supportive network of friends, family, or a therapist is essential in maintaining emotional resilience. Talking through your experiences and challenges with others can provide comfort, perspective, and encouragement, helping you manage anxiety more effectively.

5. Setting Healthy Boundaries

Setting clear boundaries in your personal, social, and professional life is an essential aspect of emotional well-being. Overcommitting or allowing yourself to be overwhelmed by external pressures can increase the likelihood of panic attacks.

a. Saying No When Necessary

Learning to say no and prioritize your well-being is an important aspect of managing stress. Setting limits on your time and energy helps prevent burnout and ensures that you can focus on your own emotional needs.

b. Managing Work and Social Stress

If work or social obligations contribute to your stress, it's important to recognize and manage these pressures. Setting realistic goals, delegating tasks, and taking regular breaks can help prevent feelings of overwhelm.

c. Communicating Your Needs

Effective communication is key to maintaining healthy relationships and preventing stress. Be open about your emotional needs with loved ones and colleagues, and be assertive in setting boundaries that protect your well-being.

6. Seeking Professional Support

While self-care strategies are important, professional help can provide additional support in preventing recurring panic attacks. Therapy, counseling, or support groups can offer valuable tools, guidance, and accountability in your ongoing recovery journey.

a. Therapy and Counseling

Working with a therapist, particularly one trained in Cognitive Behavioral Therapy (CBT), can help you build long-term strategies for preventing panic attacks. Therapy provides a safe space to explore the root causes of your anxiety and develop coping mechanisms that address both the physical and psychological aspects of panic.

b. Support Groups

Joining a support group where others share similar experiences can provide a sense of belonging and reduce feelings of isolation. In these groups, you can share your challenges and learn from others' strategies for managing anxiety.

Conclusion

Preventing panic attacks is not about avoiding all stressors, but about building emotional resilience and developing healthy habits that support your mental well-being. By recognizing early warning signs, maintaining a balanced lifestyle, and using effective coping strategies, you can significantly reduce the risk of recurring panic attacks. Keep in mind that recovery is a lifelong process, and taking proactive steps to care for your emotional health will help you lead a more balanced, fulfilling life.

Long-Term Stress Management: How to Manage Stress and Prevent Its Build-up

Chronic stress is not only exhausting but can also have significant long-term effects on both physical and mental health. Managing stress effectively over the long term requires a strategic, multifaceted approach. Here are some key techniques for managing stress and preventing it from accumulating:

1. Developing Healthy Lifestyle Habits

Consistently practicing healthy habits helps reduce the impact of stress on your body and mind. Consider these habits:

Exercise Regularly: Physical activity is one of the most effective stress relievers. Exercise releases endorphins, which improve mood, reduce anxiety, and increase energy levels. Aim for at least 30 minutes of moderate exercise most days of the week.

Sleep Hygiene: Good sleep is essential for managing stress. Aim for 7–9 hours of quality sleep each night. Establish a relaxing bedtime routine, limit screen time before bed, and create a calm, quiet sleep environment.

Healthy Diet: A balanced diet helps regulate stress hormones. Include plenty of fruits, vegetables, lean proteins, and whole grains in your diet, while limiting processed foods, caffeine, and alcohol.

2. Time Management and Prioritization

Stress often arises from feeling overwhelmed with too many responsibilities. Effective time management can alleviate that burden:

Set Boundaries: Learn to say no when necessary to avoid overcommitting yourself.

Prioritize Tasks: Use tools like to-do lists or digital planners to organize tasks by urgency and importance. Break larger tasks into smaller, manageable steps.

Take Breaks: Regular breaks during work or study time can help reduce mental fatigue and prevent burnout.

3. Mindfulness and Meditation

Mindfulness practices are effective for managing stress in the long run. Meditation, deep breathing, and mindful movement techniques like yoga can promote relaxation and help reduce feelings of anxiety.

Mindfulness Meditation: Setting aside just 10–15 minutes a day for meditation can help calm the mind and improve emotional resilience.

Deep Breathing Exercises: Simple deep breathing exercises can activate the body's relaxation response, which helps counteract stress.

4. Building Emotional Resilience
Building emotional resilience allows you to better cope with stress when it arises. This involves fostering an optimistic outlook, improving emotional regulation, and seeking social support.
Positive Thinking: Practice reframing negative thoughts into more positive or constructive ones. For example, instead of thinking "I can't handle this," try "This is tough, but I can get through it."
Emotional Regulation: Practice techniques like journaling or talking to a trusted friend to process emotions before they build up.
Seek Support: Surround yourself with a supportive social network, whether it's friends, family, or a therapist. Talking about your stress with someone you trust can provide relief and perspective.
5. Engaging in Hobbies and Interests
Taking time for activities you enjoy can help create a buffer against stress. Engage in hobbies or creative outlets such as art, reading, gardening, or volunteering. These activities can provide a mental break and improve your overall sense of well-being.
6. Setting Realistic Goals
Unrealistic expectations can lead to frustration and stress. Break large goals into smaller, achievable steps and celebrate small victories along the way. Setting realistic goals keeps stress at manageable levels and fosters a sense of accomplishment.
7. Seeking Professional Help
Sometimes, stress management requires professional intervention. Cognitive Behavioral Therapy (CBT), for example, can help individuals address the underlying thought patterns contributing to stress. Consulting a counselor or therapist can provide valuable tools and strategies for coping with chronic stress.
8. Relaxation and Stress-Relief Techniques
There are many relaxation techniques that can help reduce stress in the long term, including:
Progressive Muscle Relaxation: Tensing and relaxing muscle groups to release physical tension.
Aromatherapy: Using essential oils, such as lavender or chamomile, to promote relaxation.
Nature Walks: Spending time outdoors in natural settings can lower cortisol levels and reduce stress.

Conclusion:
Long-term stress management is about creating a lifestyle that reduces the sources of stress and builds the tools to handle it effectively when it arises. A combination of healthy habits, emotional resilience, relaxation techniques, and seeking professional help when necessary will ensure that stress does not accumulate and negatively affect your life. By staying proactive and aware of your stress triggers, you can maintain a balanced and healthy approach to managing stress over time.

Conclusion: From Panic to Peace – Success Stories and Inspiration for Those Seeking Full Recovery

Overcoming panic attacks and anxiety is a journey, one that requires patience, resilience, and the willingness to embrace change. While the path may seem daunting, countless individuals have walked this road before and emerged stronger, more at peace, and better equipped to handle life's challenges.

Success Stories: Real People, Real Triumphs

Emma's Story: Emma struggled with panic attacks for years, often feeling trapped by the fear of her next episode. It wasn't until she discovered mindfulness meditation and began regular therapy that she started to gain control. By practicing mindfulness daily and adopting cognitive-behavioral techniques, Emma found herself living a life with much fewer panic attacks, eventually managing to stop them altogether. Today, she is thriving in her career and has learned to embrace life's challenges with confidence.

James's Journey: James felt like his life was spiraling out of control as panic attacks became a constant companion. The turning point came when he realized that by seeking help and accepting that recovery was possible, he could regain his life. With the support of a compassionate therapist, James learned how to reframe his thoughts and manage stress better. Through consistent therapy, exercise, and building a supportive network of friends and family, James was able to overcome his fears and anxiety. Now, he lives without the looming threat of panic attacks and enjoys traveling and exploring new experiences.

Sophia's Path to Recovery: Sophia's panic attacks often left her feeling isolated and hopeless. But when she started journaling her emotions and practicing deep-breathing techniques, she began to notice small changes. Over time, she also integrated relaxation exercises and improved her sleep routine. As she gradually gained control over her body's responses to stress, Sophia found peace and began reconnecting with her passion for painting. Today, she is a published artist and an advocate for mental health awareness.

Inspiration for the Journey Ahead
The road from panic to peace may be long, but it is achievable. Every step you take towards understanding your triggers, learning new coping mechanisms, and seeking help is a victory. It's important to remember that recovery is not about perfection—it's about progress. Every small step forward builds your emotional resilience and helps you reclaim your life from the grip of panic. There is no one-size-fits-all solution, but with the right tools, mindset, and support, you can overcome panic attacks and anxiety. Whether through therapy, lifestyle changes, mindfulness practices, or medication, you can find a path that works for you. Above all, remember that you are not alone. Thousands of people, just like you, have experienced what you're going through and have come out stronger. Your journey is a testament to your strength and your willingness to create a healthier, more peaceful future.
Take it one day at a time, and keep moving forward. Peace is within your reach.